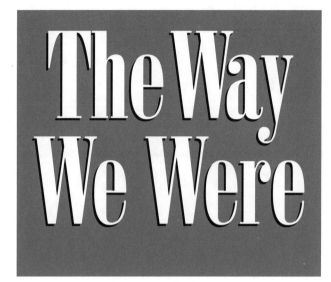

The Way We Were

BC's Amazing Journey to the Millennium

By the staff of THE Province

HARBOUR PUBLISHING

Copyright © 2000 Vancouver Province
Millennium Notebook sections copyright © 1999 Knight-Ridder
  2 3 4 5   03 02 01 00

Sources for "The Decade in BC" sections:
The Greater Vancouver Book, edited by Chuck Davis
Images of History: Twentieth Century British Columbia through the Front Pages, by William Rayner
Vancouver: An Illustrated Chronology, edited by Chuck Davis and Shirley Mooney
The 1999 Canadian Global Almanac, edited by John Robert Colombo

All rights reserved. No part of this publication may be reproduced, stored in a retrieval system or transmitted, in any form or by any means, without prior permission of the publisher or, in the case of photocopying or other reprographic copying, a licence from CANCOPY (Canadian Reprography Collective), 214 King Street West, Toronto, Ontario, M5H 3S6

Harbour Publishing
P.O. Box 219
Madeira Park, BC
Canada V0N 2H0

THE CANADA COUNCIL | LE CONSEIL DES ARTS
FOR THE ARTS | DU CANADA
SINCE 1957 | DEPUIS 1957

We acknowledge the financial support of the Government of Canada through the Book Publishing Industry Development Program for our publishing activities. We further acknowledge the support of the Canada Council for the Arts and the Province of British Columbia through the British Columbia Arts Council for our publishing program.

Edited for the house by Silas White
Design by Warren Clark

Cover captions:

Front Cover: Train and construction workers on the Kaslo and Slocan Railway trestle at Payne Bluff, 1906, BC Archives A-02592. Insets (l to r): Warren Bernard says a final goodbye to his father Jack who is heading off to war, 1940, Claud Detloff/*The Province*; rioting follows the Vancouver Canucks loss in Game 7 of the Stanley Cup final, 1994, Ric Ernst/*The Province*.

Back Cover, clockwise from top right: The Rossland Ladies' Hockey Team, 1900, courtesy Rossland Museum; snowboarder Ross Rebagliati at the Olympic Games in Nagano, 1998, courtesy Reuters; the controversial "Cary Fir" photo, 1895, Vancouver City Archives TR P8 N44.

Canadian Cataloguing in Publication Data

Main entry under title:

The way we were

  Based on articles in the *Vancouver Province* newspaper.
  ISBN 1-55017-230-1
  1. British Columbia—History. I. Title: *Province* (Vancouver, B.C.)
  FC3811.W39 2000   971.1   C00-910763-0
  F1087.W39 2000

Contents

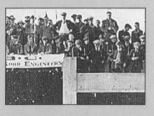

INTRODUCTION

This is the chronicle of B.C.'s amazing journey to the year 2000—the story of how ordinary people built an extraordinary province.

In this special millennium series created by Province staff, we've used lively photos and writing to chronicle everyday B.C. We've looked back at life before the Europeans arrived and at the rough-and-tumble world of the 19th century, a time of horses and wagons, of people digging for gold and building communities. And we've provided a decade-by-decade account of the last 100 years.

We spent dozens of hours in archives and searching through *Province* picture files to find the best, most engaging photographs. We sought out pictures that give a sense of time, a sense of person and place—the enduring images of everyday history.

It became a shared effort. *Province* readers sorted family photos and rummaged through dusty attics to send us treasured pictures for this, our community photo album. Our writers researched the history of the province, compiled the important official dates and found the small, telling facts and stories that show us how things really were—from the price of bread to the cost of a Point Grey bungalow in 1925.

The Way We Were was the work of about a dozen talented, hard-working people. The main designer for the series as it appeared in *The Province* was Frank Myrskog. His format was skillfully adapted for the book by Warren Clark. The chief writer was Damian Inwood, who has written other historical books about B.C. Reporters Mike Roberts, Hardip Johal and Melissa Radler also worked on the project.

Copy editor John Fuller provided indispensable help with the entire package. He had assistance from editors Bill Holden and Will Wigle. Pacific Press Librarian Kate Bird helped us find dozens of terrific photographs from Province files and Debbie Schachter of the Library assisted with our historical research. *Province* office manager Joan Fader provided help with the photos.

Doug Fischer, a friend and former colleague from the *Ottawa Citizen*, provided inspiration for the series.

We got great co-operation from people at many of the archives in B.C., particularly B.C. Archives, the staff at the Vancouver Public Library Special Collections section, City of Vancouver Archives and the Jewish Historical Society of B.C.

Thanks to former *Province* Editor Michael Cooke who believed in the project enough to give it the money and newspaper space needed to make it work.

The series was enormously successful. We sent almost 340,000 copies of *The Province* into schools for our Newspaper in Education program. And our readers were delighted with the 11-part series. Many called and asked whether the series could be reproduced in a book. Harbour Publishing agreed to do it and here it is.

We hope you enjoy it.

Ros Guggi
Project Editor,
The Province

— B.C. Archives A-00350

Spences Bridge, 1867 Two freight wagons pulled by a mule train make their way along the Cariboo Road at Great Bluff above the Thompson River. Telegraph poles carry wires, strung in 1865, as part of a proposed telegraph line from New Westminster to Europe via Alaska and Siberia. A teamster controls his team of 10 mules as the wagon train makes its way along the dusty, rock-strewn path that links the goldfields with the coast. The Royal Engineers had to blast a path through the rock wall.

FROM 'FIRST CONTACT' TO NATIONHOOD

BY DAMIAN INWOOD

A single moment on a stormy summer day in 1774 changes B.C. forever.

A Franciscan friar on the *Santiago,* the ship led by Spanish explorer Juan Perez, glimpses the mist-shrouded coast of the Queen Charlotte Islands on July 18.

Perez has orders from the viceroy of New Spain—now called Mexico—to explore the coast, but foul weather prevents him from coming ashore.

Two days later, Haida canoes paddle out to the *Santiago* and the Spanish later trade abalone and silver spoons at Nootka Sound on Aug. 8.

This "first contact" between Europeans and natives changes the West Coast forever.

Between 1774 and 1900, B.C. transforms from a wilderness to a bustling province in the Dominion of Canada.

It goes from a place where Indians hunt, trap and fish or fight inter-tribal battles, to one of mushrooming towns and cities controlled by white traders.

Along the way, Capt. James Cook, Capt. George Vancouver, Alexander Mackenzie, David Thompson and James Douglas, chief factor of the Hudson's Bay Co., leave their stamp on the land.

The Hudson's Bay Co. moves to Victoria in 1846 as sawmills and coal mines spring up on Vancouver Island.

The first judge is appointed in 1853. He is David Cameron, a clerk at the Nanaimo coalfields, who has no legal qualifications. More significantly, he is Douglas's brother-in-law, making Cameron B.C.'s first patronage appointee.

Rumours of gold on the Thompson and Fraser Rivers hit San Francisco and spark a rush north in 1858.

Cook named it New Caledonia but the territory is renamed British Columbia.

Douglas, its first governor, is sworn in at Fort Langley and levies a 10 per cent tariff on all goods bought by U.S. gold seekers. It is B.C.'s first tax.

Meanwhile, Gassy Jack Deighton opens his hotel in booming Gastown.

In 1871, B.C. officially becomes part of Canada with a population of 40,000, of which 30,000 are native Indians.

When CPR Engine 374 pulls into Vancouver in 1887, the West Coast is firmly linked to the rest of Canada.

> This "first contact" between Europeans and natives changes the West Coast forever

—Reuters

A hunter's remains remind us of how different life was before the fateful arrival of Europeans

Remarkably intact, a cedar hat was recovered near the remains of a man who lived more than 500 years ago.

KIMSQUIT, 1881
This Indian village near Bella Coola escapes the impact of European settlers until the 1870s. By the time this photograph is taken, some villagers have started adopting western styles of dress. By now, Euro-American goods have almost completely replaced local materials and influenced traditional ways of hunting, clothing and building. Decorations on the Kimsquit longhouse are typical of those found up and down the West Coast. The village is abandoned in the 1920s.

— B.C. Archives B-03569

WHEN CULTURES MERGED

BY DAMIAN INWOOD

A hunter walks across the mountains near what is now the B.C.-Yukon border.

He wears a finely woven cedar hat and skin robe and carries a wooden walking stick, a hunting spear and other tools, plus a leather pouch containing edible leaves and the remains of a fish.

The year is around 1425 and while we don't know how he meets his death, the iceman will be found in August 1999, frozen in time in a northern glacier.

At first, it's thought he may be up to 10,000 years old.

Close examination by archeologists and carbon-dating at the Royal B.C. Museum in Victoria show that he comes from between 1415 and 1445 A.D.

The world in which he lived is very different from the one we know today.

It would still be some 350 years before coast Indians would first see Europeans approach on their "floating islands" with masts like the skeletons of trees pointing skyward.

Because of his hat, it's believed that the hunter—dubbed Kwaday Dan Sinchi, or Long-Ago Person Found—may be of Tlingit descent.

If so, he may have been on a hunting trip, far from the coast, in what's now the Tatshenshini glacier.

The Tlingit, from the Alaska Panhandle and northern B.C., are one of dozens of tribal groups that have inhabited the coast since 9000 B.C.

But it is the Haida and Nootka who are first exposed to the ways of the white man in the 1770s.

1774

Spanish explorer Juan Perez is sent north from Mexico on the *Santiago* and gets to about the 55th parallel. On July 18, he sees the Queen Charlotte Islands through the fog but is unable to land. On July 20, he encounters Haida canoes and on Aug. 8 trades at Nootka Sound on what is now Vancouver Island.

1778

Captain James Cook lands at Nootka. He trades with Chief Maquinna. On board is George Vancouver, who will lead his own ship to the area 14 years later.

1788

Trader John Meares makes a deal with Maquinna for land and builds a fort at Nootka Sound.

1789

The Spanish claim the fort.

1790

The Nootka Convention is signed, giving Meares his land back and giving the British the right to trade in the Pacific.

1791

Captain George Vancouver sets out from Falmouth and sails by way of the Cape of Good Hope. Meanwhile, Spaniard Manuel Quimper sails into Sooke.

1792

Vancouver reaches Juan de Fuca Strait in May. He meets the Spanish vessels *Sutil* and *Mexicana,* captained by Dionisio Galiano and Cayetano Valdés. They explore the area. Vancouver also meets Spanish Commissioner Bodega y Quadra at Nootka but he fails to get the land back for England.

1793

Alexander Mackenzie reaches Bella Bella overland from the east.

1803

Officers and seamen aboard the American boat *Boston* are massacred by Chief Maquinna. The only survivors are armourer John Jewitt and a seaman named Thompson. Jewitt is taken as Maquinna's personal slave.

In a painting by Robert McVittie, Capt. George Vancouver arrives in the Strait of Juan de Fuca on April 29, 1792 on his ship *Discovery*. Vancouver has been here before, on board the *Endeavour* with Capt. James Cook in 1778. He later meets peacefully with the Musqueam Indians, who welcome him with cooked fish. Vancouver explores and charts Burrard Inlet and Howe Sound and sails around Vancouver Island. He eventually charts the Pacific Coast from Alaska to San Diego.

Two versions of the first meeting between natives and Capt. James Cook at Nootka Sound in 1778 show how the two cultures viewed that historic event.

Oral Nootka tradition holds that they first spy one sailor with a hooked nose and another who was a hunchback.

They tell Chief Maquinna that the two white men are transformed from a dog salmon and a humpback salmon.

The Nootka think Cook's ship is full of "fish come alive into people."

They gesture, telling Cook, "Nootka itchme, Nootka itchme," meaning "you go around the harbour."

Cook thinks they are telling him they are called Nootka.

In his journal, Cook describes the meeting this way:

> Cook's visit is mostly peaceful, but the early encounters aren't always this way

"We no sooner drew near the inlet than we found the coast to be inhabited; and at the place where we were first becalmed, three canoes came off to the ship.

"Having come pretty near us, a person in one of the two last stood up, and made a long harangue, inviting us to land, as we guessed, by his gestures.

"At the same time he kept strewing handfuls of feathers towards us; and some of his companions threw handfuls of a red dust or powder in the same manner.

"The person who played the orator wore the skin of some animal, and held, in each hand, something which rattled as he kept shaking it.

"One canoe was remarkable for a singular head, which had a bird's eye and bill, of an enormous size, painted on it; and a person who was in it, who seemed to be a Chief, was no less remarkable for his uncommon appearance; having many feathers hanging from his head, and being painted in an extraordinary manner.

"He held in his hand a carved bird of wood, as large as a pigeon, with which he rattled as the person first-mentioned had done; and was no less vociferous in his harangue, which was attended with some expressive gestures."

Cook's visit is mostly peaceful, but the early encounters aren't always this way.

In 1885, when Capt. James Hanna pays a visit to the Nootka, it almost sparks a war.

There are two versions of it.

Hanna's men blame the Nootka for stealing iron tools.

The Nootka, in turn, point to a crass practical joke by the crew of Hanna's ship, *Harmon*.

Chief Maquinna later tells Spanish explorers that he is invited on board and placed on a chair.

Under the chair is a small amount of gunpowder, with a powder trail leading from it.

When a sailor lights the trail, Maquinna's chair is thrown into the air. The chief's dignity, as well as his behind, is badly scarred.

The incident sparks a clash in which several natives are killed.

Cook and Hanna are at opposite ends of the spectrum when it comes to their dealings with native Indians.

It is the start of a time of change that will see the Indian culture diluted and tribes decimated by smallpox, influenza, tuberculosis and measles.

— B.C. Archives PDP-02252

A portrait of Capt. George Vancouver after his return to England. Vancouver also sailed with the famed Capt. James Cook.

Venereal disease spreads when chiefs give their slave women to visiting sailors.

When Cook lands, there are an estimated two to three hundred tribes scattered between the Rockies and the coast.

The native Indian population might be as high as 100,000, a figure that will drop to about 30,000 by the mid-1800s.

Trading between whites and Indians leads to the widespread use of firearms, tobacco and alcohol.

In the Interior, natives become dependent on the guns and lose the will to go back to their old ways of hunting with bows and arrows.

At this time, free-standing totem poles first become commonplace.

Until now, these carvings have graced interior house-posts but there is a greater demand for ceremonial, artistic activity.

The coastal Indians also quickly learn how to exact revenge.

In 1803, Chief Maquinna reacts angrily when he's insulted in English by an American ship's captain. Maquinna's English is good and he understands the slurs.

He invades the vessel, killing all the officers and seamen aboard except two, one of whom is made Maquinna's personal slave.

In 1811, another massacre takes place in Clayoquot Sound.

Local Indians seek revenge after a group are taken by an American whaler and left marooned off the California coast.

They board another ship, the *Tonquin*, and massacre most of the crew.

Four or five escape by boat but not before they light a slow fuse to the powder magazine.

When the ship blows up, about 200 natives die.

As "civilization" slowly takes hold in B.C., the two sides settle into an uneasy partnership, which exists to this day.

1805

Simon Fraser arrives in B.C. overland and names the area New Caledonia.

1807

David Thompson reaches the Kootenays, overland from Rocky Mountain House.

1811

David Stuart of Pacific Fur Co. sets off from Fort Astoria to build Fort Kamloops on the Thompson River.

Chief Wickaninnish massacres the crew of the *Tonquin* as revenge after 12 tribe members are left marooned in California by a U.S. whaler. Five crew escape and light a fuse on the ship, which blows up, killing 200 native Indians.

1821

The Hudson's Bay Company is formed.

1824

James McMillan comes from Fort George on the Columbia River to look for a B.C. trade route. McMillan comes into Semi-ahmoo Bay (White Rock) and follows the Nikomekl River up to Langley Prairie, which he identifies as a likely place for a trading post.

1827

Fort Langley is completed.

1828

Hudson's Bay Co. Governor George Simpson leaves York factory for a tour of New Caledonia forts. Simpson rides in his own canoe with a bagpiper and nine voyageurs with vermilion paddles. He arrives at Fort St. James and is met by James Douglas, a young clerk, who will eventually govern the territory. Simpson comes by water through the Fraser Canyon.

1835

The *Beaver*, a sturdy steam vessel, is launched in London. It sails round Cape Horn, arriving on the Columbia River in 1836. A crew of 31 includes 13 woodcutters who chop the six or seven cords of wood the ship uses each day.

1837

W.H. McNeill, captain of the *Beaver*, finds "an excellent harbour" on southeast Vancouver Island.

1839

Douglas is appointed Chief Factor of the HBC.

VANCOUVER, 1885 Samuel L. Clemens, better known as Mark Twain, is recovering from a bad cold in the Hotel Vancouver while on a speaking tour. He is almost broke and is trying to raise money to tour Australia. His visit coincides with a drought, and forest fires have left a pall of smoke over the Northwest. Twain's 10-cigar-a-day habit doesn't help. He is so hoarse he almost cancels the lecture but soldiers on, delighting a crowd of 1,200 at the Vancouver Opera House.

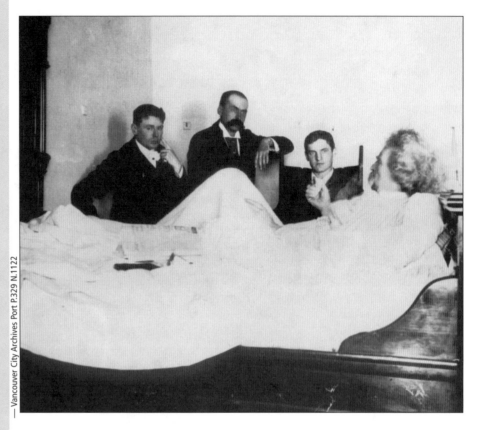

— Vancouver City Archives Port P.329 N.1122

— B.C. Archives A-00347

CAMELS IN B.C.

The strangest pack animals to work B.C.'s goldfields are Bactrian camels from central Asia. Twenty-three of these "ships of the desert" are shipped from Arizona to San Francisco and on to Victoria to work the Cariboo gold rush of 1862.

They belong to Frank Laumeister, a veteran U.S. gold miner, who pays $6,000 for them.

Laumeister thinks his camels will be able to go six to 10 days without water and travel 50 to 70 kilometres a day with a 500-kilogram load.

In fact, the camels never carry more than 300 kilograms, and the rocky paths of the Cariboo soon tear up their feet, even after canvas and rawhide boots are made for them.

As well, pack horses, mules and donkeys get spooked by these strange, evil-smelling beasts. Some jump off a narrow, winding track, taking their loads to the bottom of a canyon.

A miner named John Morris, passing Quesnel Forks, sees what he thinks is a large grizzly bear and blasts it with his rifle.

When the animal topples over, Morris discovers it is one of Laumeister's camels with a gaping hole in its side.

— B.C. Archives A-03687

FORT STEELE, 1887 The North West Mounted Police set up camp at Galbraith's ferry after a dispute between settlers and the Ktunaxa people in the East Kootenays leads to fear of an uprising. It comes to a head after a local constable arrests two Indians for the 1884 murder of two white miners. Settlers call for help, and Supt. Samuel Benfield Steele travels from Fort McLeod, Alta., with three officers and 75 men. Steele establishes a fort and settles the dispute before leaving in 1888.

1842

Douglas goes to the Vancouver Island port. It is originally called Fort Camosun, an Indian name, then Fort Albert after the prince consort, then Fort Victoria after the young Queen Victoria.

1846

On June 15, boundary is agreed as the 49th parallel from the Rockies to the coast, with Britain retaining all of Vancouver Island.

1848

First sawmill in B.C. is built at Fort Victoria.

1849

Coal mining begins after seams are found on the east coast of Vancouver Island.

1850

Richard Blanshard, a lawyer, arrives in Victoria to take up the post of colonial governor. He appoints a legislative council before returning to England a bitter man after being one-upped by Douglas, the uncompromising HBC chief. Douglas becomes governor of the colony.

1853

The first judge, David Cameron, is appointed. He has no qualifications and has been a clerk in the coalfields. He is also Douglas's brother-in-law.

1856

The first legislative assembly of seven representatives is elected.

1857

HBC officers at Fort Kamloops report finding gold in the Thompson River. Gold mining licences cost one pound, one shilling.

1858

Rumours of gold on the Thompson and the Fraser hit San Francisco and the rush is on. A Bill making the mainland a Crown colony is passed in London. To avoid confusion with land in the South Pacific named New Caledonia by Capt. Cook, the new colony will be called British Columbia. Douglas bans firearms, ammunition and liquor from U.S. boats going up the Fraser and imposes a 10-per-cent tariff on all goods. It is B.C.'s first tax. Douglas is appointed governor of the new colony at a salary of £1,800 to govern both Vancouver Island and the Mainland. The first newspaper, called the *British Colonist*, starts publishing in Victoria.

— City of Surrey Archives 21.31

SURREY, 1887 Relatives, friends and neighbours help in a barn-raising on the MacKenzie farm in Clover Valley, later known as Cloverdale. Duncan and Isabella MacKenzie have five daughters and seven sons and move to B.C. from Ontario in 1882. They set up a homestead in Surrey in 1883, where they live and are active in school, community, municipal and provincial affairs.

— Vancouver City Archives CAN P47 N229

VANCOUVER, 1887 Thousands of Vancouver residents gather to greet the arrival of the first passenger train from Montreal. The day is May 23, 1887, the eve of Queen Victoria's golden jubilee. Engine 374 puffs into the CPR station after travelling on the newly built, 19-kilometre extension from Port Moody. The engine, built in Montreal in 1886, is now on display in Vancouver at the Roundhouse Community Centre.

THE GOLD RUSH

BY DAMIAN INWOOD

In 1858, the Cariboo gold rush sparks B.C. into life. More than 20,000 hard-bitten miners pour into the colony from San Francisco when rumours of rich gold strikes reach their ears.

The claims have run dry in California, and Fort Victoria is just a few hundred miles by boat.

The resulting influx leads to Victoria blossoming almost overnight from a fur-traders' stockade into a booming city of thousands.

Billy Barker strikes pay dirt on the banks of Williams Creek in 1862.

Within a year, Barkerville has a population of more than 10,000 and is one of the biggest cities in Western Canada.

One claim alone pays a yield of 409 ounces in a single day, worth $6,544—a small fortune.

Barkerville attracts the usual gold-field dregs—gamblers, prostitutes, thieves and conmen.

Law and order prevails under the

— B.C. Archives F-00305

famous "hanging judge," Matthew Baillie Begbie.

The city doesn't lack for culture.

It boasts its own library and places where more cultured folk can listen to opera and classical music.

The tinder-dry town of wooden buildings is hit by fire on Sept. 16, 1868, sparked in gold-rush style.

A miner tries to steal a kiss from a dancing girl who is ironing her dress at the back of a saloon.

He knocks over a stovepipe.

About 80 minutes later only one building remains, but a new town springs up immediately.

BARKERVILLE, 1868 This booming town boasts 10,000 miners, all drawn by the search for the motherlode. Since 1862, when Billy Barker strikes pay dirt, the town has been a magnet for all the flotsam and jetsam of the California goldfields. This is the main street just before the town burns down on Sept. 16, 1868.

— B.C. Archives A-00515

VICTORIA, 1895 Victoria, given a kick-start by the Cariboo gold rush in the 1860s, has another boom when miners rush to the Klondike. B. Williams & Co. on Johnson Street is just one of many to cash in. The store started out as a clothier and hatter but quickly transformed to Klondyke Outfitters when the Yukon gold rush started. The store offers everything from sleds and snowshoes to packs marked "Dawson City via Skagway."

1859

Col. Richard Clemens Moody, B.C. land commissioner, decides Fort Langley is too vulnerable to attack and chooses a hilly town site downriver called Queensborough as the mainland's capital. It is later known as New Westminster.

1860

Rich gold finds at Horsefly lead to the Cariboo gold rush.

1862

Victoria gets a city charter.

1864

The last bastion of Fort Victoria is demolished and Douglas leaves office. Frederick Seymour takes over.

Thirteen die in the Chilcotin War, near Quesnel, after Indians attack a ferryman, work crew and pack train.

1866

Vancouver Island and the mainland become one colony.

1867

The Dominion of Canada is proclaimed.

1868

A meeting is held and proposes B.C. seek admission to Canada. The legislative council decides to leave Queensborough for Victoria.

1868

Fire destroys Barkerville.

1869

Seymour dies of dysentry. Anthony Musgrave replaces him as governor.

1870

Sir George Etienne Cartier offers B.C. a trans-Canada railway to be started in two years and completed in 10.

1871

The province of B.C. becomes part of Canada.

1874

A small revolution breaks out in Victoria over Ottawa's broken railway promises.

1875

Ottawa offers to fund the Esquimalt and Nanaimo Railway instead.

1876

The offer is rejected and a motion for B.C. to secede from Canada passes by 14 to nine, but is never acted upon.

— Vancouver City Archives BU P403 N387

VANCOUVER, 1884 The Wah Chong family runs a Chinese laundry on the south side of Water Street between Abbott and Carrall streets in Gastown in 1884. Behind the building is an eight-hectare clearing, full of blackberry bushes, skunk cabbage and logging debris. At night, deer often clatter across the sidewalk where the Chong family is posing. Jennie Wah Chong is the first Asian to attend school in Vancouver.

VANCOUVER, 1898 These bathing belles are getting ready for a swim at Greer's Beach, now known as Kits Beach, near the foot of Yew Street. By-laws at the time ban swimming or bathing in public without a bathing suit extending from the neck to the knees. Greer's Beach is named after the first white settler, Sam Greer, who lived there from 1882 to 1890, when he lost a dispute with the Canadian Pacific Railway over title to the land. Greer went to jail for shooting and wounding the sheriff who came to evict him.

— Vancouver City Archives BE P67 N29

— Vancouver City Archives TR P8 N44

THE BIG HOAX

This forest behemoth is supposed to have been felled in Lynn Valley in 1895. In fact, it is one of the most successful hoaxes ever pulled on our neighbours to the south.

In 1895, a group of lumbermen in Seattle forms a club called the "Concatenated Order of Hoo-Hoo."

A branch club in Vancouver invites the Seattle fellows to visit and proceeds to loudly proclaim that B.C. can grow bigger trees than Washington State.

They produce this photograph to prove it.

It represents a giant fir, said to measure 417 feet high, its trunk 25 feet across and its circumference 77 feet.

The fake photograph is so well done that it is widely reproduced in official forestry journals and even by the Dominion government in Ottawa.

Who's behind it?

No one ever owns up, but the prime suspect is George Cary, a pioneer who comes to Vancouver in 1886 and cuts the first trail up Lonsdale Avenue towards Grouse Mountain.

He later denies the suggestion that he is the man standing on the ladder in the photo.

James McWhinney, logging boss for many years at Moodyville Sawmill, confirms that "no such tree ever grew in B.C."

And another old timer, an N. Pearson, spends a lot of time unsuccessfully trying to locate the log and its stump.

How was the hoax perpetrated?

Close examination of the photograph shows ghostly outlines around some of the figures, suggesting that they have simply been cut out and pasted onto a photo of a much smaller log.

The easiest one to spot is the man sitting top right. The right side of his legs shows signs of the forgery.

And the man holding a child, at top left, seems to be standing on thin air with his right foot.

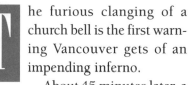

— Vancouver Public Library, Special Collections 1089

THE VANCOUVER FIRE

BY DAMIAN INWOOD

The furious clanging of a church bell is the first warning Vancouver gets of an impending inferno.

About 45 minutes later, a city of 1,000 wooden buildings is just a charred field of wreckage.

About 20 lives are lost in the gale-whipped blaze, which spreads from fires set by crews clearing CPR land nearby.

It is Sunday, June 13, 1886, and fire breaks out at about 2:15 p.m.

As the bells of St. James Church ominously toll at the corner of Powell Street and what's now Main Street, residents screaming, "Fire! Fire!" run from their homes.

Sheets of flame leap from tree to tree just south of the city and sidewalks are quickly engulfed.

A huge flame, 30 metres long, bursts from "Gassy Jack" Deighton's hotel and swallows up buildings across Maple Tree Square, where the Europe Hotel stands today.

Frightened citizens run, but some are trapped in the furnace.

Others head to the waterfront, where loggers build makeshift rafts.

Bedraggled survivors are eventually ferried across to Moodyville—what is now North Vancouver—where they helplessly watch the smoking ruins of a once-bustling town.

By the next morning, tents and buildings are springing up.

On June 16, a meeting of council takes place in a tent to plan for the rebirth of the city (pictured top left).

It's a scene that's repeated in other communities of wooden homes and businesses in the days before fire departments, hydrants or water supplies.

Barkerville is burned to the ground in 1868, and New Westminster's downtown business district is ravaged by fire in 1898.

B.C. PRE-1900

1885
The last spike is driven in the Canadian Pacific Railway at Craigellachie, between Revelstoke and Kamloops.

1886
The city of Vancouver incorporates but is then destroyed by fire.

1887
The first passenger train pulls into Vancouver from Montreal.

1897
The Klondike gold rush begins.

1898
The Province begins publishing in Vancouver.

–Damian Inwood

NEW WESTMINSTER, 1898 Smoking ruins are all that's left of downtown New Westminster the morning after a devastating fire. The Columbia Street fire, which struck on the night of Sept. 10, 1898, gutted buildings and houses in the central business district. The city market, salmon canneries, Canadian Pacific Navigation warehouse and studio of photographer Stephen Thompson, who took this picture, were all destroyed.

— B.C. Archives A-03363

—B.C. Archives NA-42000

Vancouver, 1909 Ladies and gentlemen turn out on horseback, in carriages, in cars and on foot for the opening of the second Granville Street Bridge. The first bridge, built in 1889, was made of timber and wire ropes and cost $16,000.

A BURST OF GROWTH

BY DAMIAN INWOOD

As calendars click over to 1900, B.C., Canada and the world enter an era of enormous change.

The first decade sees breakthroughs such as the Wright brothers' first manned flight, Marconi's first trans-Atlantic wireless signal and Einstein's first steps in atomic theory.

In B.C., it is a time of unprecedented growth, with Vancouver rising from the ashes of the 1886 fire and blossoming to more than 25,000 people by 1900.

The inner mind is also under the public microscope as psychologist Sigmund Freud tells us that dreams are the "royal road to the unconscious" in his 1900 book *The Interpretation of Dreams.*

As Canada's population reaches 5,371,315 in 1901, in Trenton, N.J., the Eastman Kodak Co. incorporates to produce Kodak cameras and photographic supplies. The Kodak Brownie sells for $1.

What's believed to be Canada's first permanent cinema, the Edison Electric Theatre, opens in Vancouver in 1902.

The first sign of a labour movement that would become a hallmark of the B.C. workplace is seen among fishermen sailing from ports along the Fraser River and in the coal mines on Vancouver Island.

The Tories, led by Richard McBride, win the 1903 B.C. election. His enemies dub the 33-year-old "Glad-Hand Dick" but his affable manner wins him friends at home and in Ottawa.

McBride faces an early test, just 17 days into his term, with the Alaska Panhandle boundary dispute.

Indignation runs high in B.C. when the British representative on an international tribunal sides with the Americans over inlets Canada is claiming.

McBride condemns the decision, which later is credited with turning many B.C. residents from thinking of themselves as British to being full-fledged Canadians.

The issue of women's rights—particularly the right to vote—gains a high profile around the world.

In 1903, Emmeline Pankhurst founds the Women's Social and Political Union in London. She campaigns under the slogan "Votes for Women" and she and her followers chain themselves to railings as part of their campaign.

Meanwhile, Madame Marie Curie discovers radiation and becomes the first woman to win a Nobel Prize.

In Toronto, in 1907, Canada Dry ginger ale is patented by chemist and pharmacist John J. McLaughlin.

And in 1909, Canadian Tommy Ryan invents five-pin bowling, which now claims to be "Canada's largest participant sport."

> In B.C., it is a time of unprecedented growth

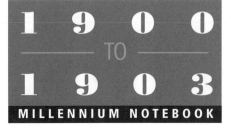

1900

Jan. 1: Vancouver enters the new century with optimism.

"At the opening of this year 1900, the people of Vancouver have good reason to look backwards with satisfaction and forward with hope," writes *Vancouver Province* editor W.C. Nichol in the first paper of the New Year.

April 26: A raging fire reduces Ottawa and Hull to ashes. Property losses are $15 million and 12,000 people lose their homes.

Sept. 8: A hurricane sweeps out of the Gulf of Mexico onto Galveston, Tex., killing more than 6,000 people. For fear of the plague, corpses are piled on the beach and burnt.

Dec. 6: The first credit union in North America is founded by Alphonse Desjardins in Quebec. Today, credit unions serve more than 4.5 million Canadians with more than 300 branches in Ontario and 79 branches in B.C.

1901

March 9: Japanese-Canadians win the right to vote under an appeal to the B.C. Elections Act but political obstruction means they don't actually get to vote until the late 1940s.

Sept. 6: U.S. President William McKinley is shot twice in the abdomen at point-blank range by anarchist Leon Czolgosz as the president stands in a receiving line at the Pan-American exposition in Buffalo, N.Y. He seems to recover but dies Sept. 14 of gangrene, whispering the words of his favourite hymn, "Nearer, my God, to Thee." Vice-President Theodore Roosevelt is president at age 42.

Oct. 24: Thousands of amazed spectators watch as Anna Edson Taylor, 43, becomes the first person to go over Niagara Falls in a barrel. Suffering only from shock and minor cuts, she advises: "Don't try it."

Dec. 10: The king of Sweden and the Norwegian Nobel Committee award the first Nobel Prizes, named after Swedish industrialist Alfred Nobel, who invented

— U.S. National Air and Space Museum

"The problem of aerial navigation without the use of a balloon has been solved at last."
—Norfolk Virginian-Pilot

Orville Wright

Wilbur Wright

Two bicycle mechanics make history

On a blustery Dec. 17, 1903, near Kill Devil Hill at Kitty Hawk, N.C., Orville and Wilbur Wright astound a few onlookers with a manned flight in a heavier-than-air, mechanically propelled airplane. The brothers, bicycle mechanics from Dayton, Ohio, achieve their breakthrough in a kite-like contraption powered by a 12-horsepower motorcycle engine.

"Not many were willing to face the rigours of a cold December wind in order to see, as they no doubt thought, another flying machine not fly," the Wrights recall later.

Onlookers are mildly impressed when Orville Wright, in his first flight, covers 37 metres in 12 airborne seconds. The brothers take turns and a fourth flight, manned by Wilbur Wright, is officially recorded as 59 seconds, covering a distance of 260 metres.

dynamite. Among the first winners is Wilhelm Roentgen of Germany for discovering X-rays.

1902

March 18: Italian tenor Enrico Caruso makes his first phonograph recordings in a hotel room in Milan. He records 10 songs for $500 US.

May 8: Saint-Pierre, capital of Martinique, is destroyed by the eruption of Mount Pelee. All 25,400 residents die, except one, a Mr. Cyparis, in jail for drunkenness.

May 24: The first Victoria Day is observed throughout Canada, 16 months after Queen Victoria's death. Prime Minister Wilfrid Laurier designates the public holiday to fall on May 24, the Queen's birthday. In 1952, it changes to the Monday before May 25.

May 31: The Boer War ends with a treaty signing at Vereeniging, South Africa.

1903

April 24: The New York Stock Exchange's new building at Broad and Wall streets is dedicated amid a blizzard of tickertape.

Aug. 14: A claim is filed on the richest silver vein in the world, at Cobalt, Ont., attracting 10,000 people to mine $80 million in ore.

Nov. 17: At a congress in London, Russia's Social Democratic Labour Party splits into two—the moderate Mensheviks ("minority") and the radical Bolsheviks ("majority"). Vladimir Ilyich Lenin, fiery young leader of the Bolsheviks, advocates the destruction of capitalism and establishment of an international socialist state.

Enrico Caruso

MESSAGES WITHOUT WIRES

On Dec. 12, 1901, Guglielmo Marconi receives the first trans-Atlantic wireless message as he sits in a hut on the cliffs at St. John's, Nfld.

An English telegrapher, 2,735 kilometres away in Poldhu, Cornwall, taps out the letter "S" and Marconi picks it up on a crude receiver with a kite antenna.

"I now felt, for the first time, absolutely certain that the day would come," writes Marconi at the time, "when mankind would be able to send messages without wires, not only across the Atlantic but between the farthermost ends of the Earth."

PASSAGES

QUEEN VICTORIA

Queen Victoria, who has been on the British throne since 1837, dies Jan. 22, 1901, at Cowes on the Isle of Wight at age 82.

At her death, the British Empire is at its height, with outposts on five continents and an enormous navy to protect its trade routes. Most of her subjects have known no other monarch. Victoria is succeeded by her 59-year-old son, Albert Edward, Prince of Wales, who ushers in the nine-year Edwardian period as Edward VII.

MUSIC

RAGTIME'S ALL THE RAGE

Scott Joplin, born to freed slaves in 1868 in Bowie County, near Texarkana, Texas, is riding a wave of popularity as the "King of Ragtime." The ragtime genre, with its syncopated rhythm, was already established when Joplin's "Original Rags" was published in early 1899. But "Maple Leaf Rag," also published in 1899, becomes so successful that it captures the ear of the North American public in the first years of the new century.

FOOD

THE HOT DOG

Until 1906, fatty sausages served on long buns sliced lengthwise had names such as frankfurters, red hots, dachshund sausages and wienies.

But Hearst sports cartoonist Thomas Aloysius (Tad) Dorgan is credited with giving the ballpark snack the name "hot dog."

Dorgan is already depicting Germans as talking dachshunds. Playing off an urban legend that sausages sold at Coney Island and the Polo Grounds contain dog meat, Dorgan draws a vendor peddling a dachshund, slathered in mustard, in a bun. The caption reads: "Get your hotdogs."

BOOKS

ANNE OF GREEN GABLES

Lucy Maud Montgomery's first novel, *Anne of Green Gables,* is an instant best-seller in 1908.

The carrot-topped heroine becomes a world-famous literary character and single-handedly puts Prince Edward Island on the map.

Montgomery goes on to write seven equally popular sequels.

PASSAGES

GERONIMO

On Feb. 17, 1909, Apache chief Geronimo, who led raids against white settlers from 1858 until surrendering in 1886, dies of pneumonia at Fort Sill, Okla., aged 80.

Geronimo is an international celebrity, attending the St. Louis World's Fair in 1904.

"Now there are very few of us left," he says, just before he dies.

RECORDS

SPEED, SIZE AND GRACE

On Sept. 13, 1907, the Cunard liner *SS Lusitania* arrives in New York on its maiden voyage, setting a record of five days, 54 minutes, for the trans-Atlantic crossing from Queenstown, Ireland. The 28,600-tonne *Lusitania* is 241 metres long and can carry 2,000 passengers and 600 crew, the largest liner yet.

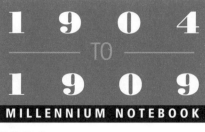

1904 TO 1909
MILLENNIUM NOTEBOOK

1904

Feb. 8: Japanese naval forces launch a stunning night attack against the Russian fleet off Port Arthur in southern Manchuria, starting the biggest war thus far in history and the first in which armoured battleships, torpedoes, land mines and modern machine guns will be used.

May 5: Denton True (Cyclone) Young, better known as Cy Young, pitches the first perfect game in major-league baseball, for the Boston Pilgrims against the Philadelphia Athletics.

Nov. 3: Wilfrid Laurier is re-elected prime minister in a Liberal landslide.

Nov. 15: King C. Gillette is granted a patent for a razor with a disposable blade. Razor and blade sales skyrocket.

1905

Feb. 23: At 37, Paul P. Harris has been a cowboy, actor, reporter, merchant, coal dealer and mining engineer. Now, as a civic-minded lawyer in bustling Chicago, he meets with three friends to form a community service organization. They agree to meet in rotation at one another's downtown offices, spawning the group's name—the Rotary Club.

Sept. 1: Alberta and Saskatchewan become Canada's eighth and ninth provinces.

Dec. 5: Roald Amundsen reaches Eagle City, Alaska, by dogsled with news that,

Laurier

Miner

with his ship *Gjoa* stuck in the ice, he has become the first person to navigate the Northwest Passage.

1906

Feb. 23: Canadian Tommy Burns, born Noah Brusso, wins the world heavyweight boxing championship in Los Angeles in a gruelling 20-round decision over Marvin Hart. He loses the title in 1908 to Jack Johnson.

March 7: Finland becomes the first country to give women the vote, decreeing universal suffrage for citizens over the age of 24.

April 18: At 5:13 a.m., San Franciscans are jolted from their beds by a violent trembling of the earth. Fires are fed by broken gas mains. Soon, everyone is either fleeing the flames, seeking missing relatives, or helping with relief efforts.

The fires rage for three days, destroying two-thirds of the city of about 400,000. Researchers estimate that 3,000 died.

Hundreds of thousands more are homeless and 28,000 buildings are destroyed. Property damage is $400 million US.

May 8: Bill Miner, the "Gentleman Bandit," robs a train near Kamloops and is captured by the Royal Northwest Mounted Police. In 1907, he escapes from a New Westminster prison and continues bank robbing in the United States until his final incarceration in a Georgia prison. In 1982, a Canadian film of his life, *The Grey Fox,* is an international hit.

Dec. 24: Wireless operators on ships off New England are puzzled to hear a man's voice coming through equipment normally used to send and receive Morse code.

No one has ever heard a voice or music broadcast before. The man reads the Christmas story from the Gospel of Luke, then plays a violin solo and a recording of Handel's "Largo."

He is engineer Reginald Fessenden, who in 1901 patented a way of transmitting radio waves to carry natural sounds rather than chirps of code.

1907

Feb. 24: The *New York Times* publishes a list of the world's richest people. Topping

— Associated Press

Einstein explains energy

The world becomes infinitely more complicated in 1905. That's when an obscure 26-year-old patent clerk in Bern, Switzerland, publishes his musings in the German physics journal *Annalen der Physik*. He is Albert Einstein and he sets out "a simple and consistent theory of the electrodynamics of moving bodies." It becomes known as "the special theory of relativity." Einstein suggests that energy and mass are not separate and distinct, as scientists long assumed, but interact with each other and that energy has mass. He introduces history's most famous equation, $E=mc^2$ (energy equals mass times the speed of light squared). Einstein suggests that energy is contained in matter, even such tiny particles as the atom. He links space, time, matter and energy in ways never before imagined. "I have no special gift," Einstein says. "I am only passionately curious."

it is John D. Rockefeller, whose worth is estimated at $300 million US.

June 10: Five automobiles leave Peking, China (now Beijing), on a 12,900-kilometre trip to Paris crossing the Great Wall of China, the Gobi Desert and the Ural Mountains. On Aug. 10, Prince Borghese of Italy wins the race in 62 days.

July 29: Sir Robert Baden-Powell, a celebrated British general, recruits 22 boys for a field test of his essay "Boy Scouts—A Suggestion." The aim of the two-week excursion into the woods of Brownsea Island is to instil a sense of community service, chivalry and physical fitness.

Aug. 29: The Quebec Bridge, near Quebec City, collapses close to completion, killing 75 workers.

Dec. 10: Rudyard Kipling, author of *The Jungle Book,* is awarded the Nobel Prize for literature.

1908

March 29: *Mutt and Jeff,* in William Randolph Hearst's *San Francisco Examiner,* is the first comic strip to appear daily. Cartoonist Harry Conway (Bud) Fisher, then 23, will continue the strip until his death in 1954.

May 10: The first Mother's Day is observed in Philadelphia and in Grafton, W.Va., to honor the memory of Anna Reese Jarvis and American mothers living and dead. The observance is the idea of Anna M. Jarvis, daughter of Anna Reese Jarvis.

Oct. 1: The Model T rolls off Henry Ford's Detroit assembly line and becomes "a motorcar for the multitudes." The car is dubbed the Tin Lizzie because "Lizzie" is an all-purpose name for a domestic servant and the Model T has a flimsy, tinny look. The Model T's top speed is only 65 kilometres per hour but the car has good acceleration and its high clearance is perfect for the rutted, unpaved roads of the time.

Dec. 28: More than 200,000 people are killed in an earthquake with the epicentre at Messina in Sicily. There is $1 billion in property damage.

1909

Jan. 1: Men and women over 70 draw the first old-age pensions in London, England.

April 6: The third time proves lucky for explorer Robert E. Peary. Having failed twice, Peary sets out from the United States in July 1908, winters in Greenland and dashes to the North Pole. African-American Matthew Henson plants the American flag at 90 degrees north latitude on April 6, 1909.

July 25: Frenchman Louis Bleriot, 37, flies across the English Channel in 43 minutes. His 24-horsepower monoplane won £1,000, flying from Calais to Dover.

Dec. 4: The first Grey Cup game is held, with the University of Toronto defeating Toronto Parkdale Canoe Club 26-6.

Model T Ford: 1908

— Chilliwack Museum and Archives P584

CHILLIWACK, 1905 A parade passes the Henderson Block in Five Corners, now Chilliwack. The white building, built by town resident A.C. Henderson, was a famous Five Corners landmark. Henderson operated his dry goods store on the ground floor, while civic and church meetings were held on the second level.

—Ivar N. Austin / Pacific Press Library

Opposite: **PAYNE BLUFF, 1906** Workers check a new trestle on the Kaslo and Slocan Railway, a three-foot-gauge narrow railroad that operated between 1892 and about 1910. Keeping the 47-kilometre line open is always a battle against nature, with slides knocking out the link between lead, zinc and silver mines in the Sandon area and Kaslo on Kootenay Lake.

VANCOUVER, 1906 Squamish Chief Joe Capilano marches down Hastings Street, celebrating Earl Grey's first visit to the city as governor general. During this period the chief went to London to present a petition to King Edward VII about aboriginal rights and land settlement. He was accompanied by Cowichan and Cariboo chiefs and was received hospitably by the King and Queen. Capilano said after the visit he'd been warned that such matters could take up to five years to settle.

1900

The first regular ferry starts between North Vancouver and the south shore of Burrard Inlet. *North Vancouver No. 1* later becomes a private home, beached on a small island near Tofino.

A strike by fishermen from 47 canneries on the Lower Fraser is blamed in part on depleted salmon stocks due to the use of fish traps in Washington state. Hostility erupts between the white fishermen's union and Japanese fishermen who live in cannery houses.

The Dewdney Trunk Road is built on the north bank of the Fraser River.

On June 30, B.C. had 42 schools with 1,568 students on the rolls.

1901

The Union Mine in Cumberland explodes, killing 64 miners.

Vancouver's first Royal visit: the Duke and Duchess of Cornwall and York.

The census records the population of North Vancouver as 365. Meanwhile, B.C.'s population has soared in the last 10 years to 178,657, up from just 98,173 in 1891.

1902

The first CPR passenger train arrives in Steveston to serve the canneries. It becomes known as the *Sockeye Express.*

Woodward's department store opens at Hastings and Abbott streets on Sept. 12.

1903

The Carnegie Library opens at Hastings and Main Street.

H. Hooper is Vancouver's first cabbie.

The population of Delta is 2,000, of which 350 are Chinese.

1904

The first bridge across the Fraser River opens, joining New Westminster to Brownsville (North Surrey). Hailed as the engineering feat of the century, it costs $1 million.

It carries trains on the lower span, vehicles and pedestrians on the upper, which is just wide enough for two hay wagons to pass.

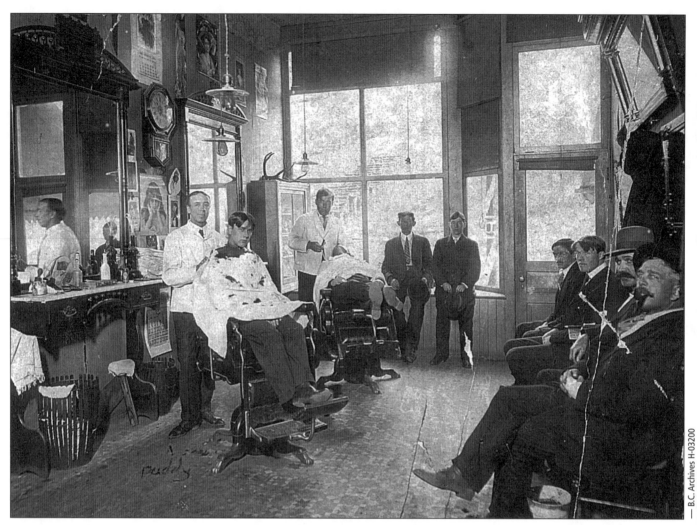

— B.C. Archives H-03200

PHOENIX, CIRCA 1900 Townsmen meet at L.R. Puddy Barber Shop in Phoenix. Copper was discovered in this southern B.C. mining town in the 1880s but by the First World War, Phoenix was a ghost town.

— B.C. Archives A-08897

FERNIE, 1908 A devastating fire swept through Fernie on Aug. 1, killing 18 people. Crow's Nest Pass coal mines, the largest industry in the district, lost almost $200,000. Only one house was saved in Fernie Annex. Here are some of the refugee homes.

— Fort Steele Heritage Town Archives FS 5.49

FORT STEELE, 1902 Townsmen shoot the breeze in the Windsor Hotel bar. Three years later, Fort Steele was a ghost town after the government bypassed it and built a railway line through nearby Cranbrook.

— Vancouver City Archives BR P59 N48 #1

CAPILANO CANYON, 1905 Peering off the edge of the Capilano Suspension Bridge, well-frocked ladies and gentlemen enjoy a close-up view of Capilano Canyon. At the turn of the century, approximately 700 visitors per year tip-toed across the rickety bridge, which was open every summer weekend, weather permitting. The first bridge was built in 1889 from rope and cedar planks. In 1904, it was replaced by a second suspension bridge, pictured here, which was reinforced with steel cables for extra safety. Today, more than 800,000 visitors per year cross the third suspension bridge, which was built to last in 1956.

1905

An eight-room house on Harwood Street in Vancouver's West End costs $3,500.

The first buildings go up at Colony Farm, which later supplies the nearby "hospital of the mind," Riverview.

The first bathhouse is built at Stanley Park for $6,000. It becomes a popular spot for the new pastime of swimming, under the watchful eye of lifeguard and swimming instructor Joe Fortes.

1906

The Smith butchering machine takes the place of a 30-man crew of Chinese cannery workers.

Alfred Wallace opens his first shipyard in North Vancouver. Burrard Dry Dock becomes the North Shore's largest industry.

1907

The Vancouver Stock Exchange is incorporated.

A rally protesting the influx of Asian immigrants turns ugly as a mob rampages through Vancouver's Chinatown and Japantown.

The first gas station in Canada opens at Cambie and Smithe streets.

1908

UBC is founded.

The Empress Hotel opens in Victoria.

B.C.'s first agricultural fair is held in New Westminster. Fraser Valley fruit is being shipped worldwide.

1909

The first export shipment of grain is made out of Vancouver.

Longshoremen strike for higher wages— 35 cents an hour for day work and 40 cents an hour for night work.

The 13-storey Dominion Trust Building at Hastings and Cambie is Vancouver's first skyscraper. It is the most modern office building in Canada. Its architect slips on the stairs and falls to his death down the building's central core.

The wreck of a Great Northern Railway work train kills 22 Japanese in the Sapperton area.

— Prince Rupert City and Regional Archives

PRINCE RUPERT, 1907 Dining out is a new luxury in turn-of-the-century Prince Rupert—a meal at the Dominion Restaurant costs 25 cents.

MALCOLM ISLAND, 1905 For Province reader Trevis Hilton Holmes' grandparents, Sunday afternoon was a time for rest, relaxation, and bird shooting. Dressed in their Sunday best in 1905, Holmes' grandparents (couple at left) proudly display the catch of the day—a bald eagle—along with other family members. The Hilton family emigrated from Finland in 1900 and settled in Sointula on Malcolm Island in the Alert Bay area.

— B.C. Archives C-07348

BAMFIELD, 1907 The centre of the British Empire is … Bamfield, on the west coast of Vancouver Island. The Bamfield Island Cable Station is the centre of the British Empire's telegraph system, and plays an important role in the Allies' communication during the two world wars. The station can cable 34,560 words in 24 hours. It takes 27.9 seconds to transmit the letter 's' across the Pacific Ocean to Australia.

Bamfield was originally built as a small station along the West Coast Trail that guided shipwrecked sailors to safety.

FORT LANGLEY, 1900 Twenty-year-old Laura Mavis, the great aunt of Province reader Bruce Mavis, and her dog Toby admire a view of Macmillan Island from her family's Fort Langley home. Laura's father, Francis Alexander Mavis, struck it rich in the California gold rush, and was headed for the Fraser River to test his luck when he was sidetracked by land for sale. Mavis bought 185 acres, including Fort Langley, from the Hudson's Bay Company on Jan. 31, 1888, for a whopping $5,850. In 1923 Mavis sold what is now the Fort Langley Historical Site to the government.

— Rossland Museum

ROSSLAND, 1900 The Rossland Ladies' Hockey Team stands poised and ready for action at the Rossland Skating Rink. The team—formed on Feb. 2, 1900, in the young town founded by Ross Thompson in 1892—was brought together for a match during the Rossland Winter Carnival. They beat a Nelson ladies' team 4-0 Feb. 17.

VICTORIA, 1902 Horse racing was a popular spectator sport in turn-of-the-century Victoria. At the Willows race track in 1902, wealthy and idle young men eye their favourite equestrians. The Exhibition Building, built with the track in 1890, stands gloriously in the background. The Oak Bay building boasted 20,000 square feet of floor space, two staircases, and an open balcony 75 feet off the ground. It was destroyed by fire in December, 1907.

— B.C. Archives A-08024

— Vancouver Public Library, Special Collections 1260

VANCOUVER, 1909 Couples swirl around a Vancouver dance hall. The introduction of paved streets in the 1900s meant that a lady could now walk down a city street without getting her hem dirty.

VANCOUVER, 1902
A Vancouver General Hospital ambulance is ready for service in 1902. The carriage, donated by the Women's Auxiliary, was driven by Dick Woodrow.

VANCOUVER, CIRCA 1909 Pausing for a break, workers lay cement sidewalks at Georgia near Seymour in downtown Vancouver. In political debates of the time, the city's engineering department was often criticized for its lack of efficiency.

— Vancouver General Hospital PR69100

— Vancouver Public Library Special Collections 6751

About work in wards

Editor Province —

I see in your paper of August 31 that the city is complaining about not being able to get enough men to work in the different wards. Now I have been to the foreman of Ward Five and he tells me that he has all the men he wants. He will go downtown and hire men to work for him, while there are a number of men in Ward Five who are taxpayers and who cannot get a day's work from the foreman, Mr. Woods, and for my part I would like to know the reason why, but I think it is because he has some pets around him. Please publish this letter and oblige.

A Reader of The Province
Vancouver, Sept. 2, 1905

Sabbath and man

Editor Province —

It is reported that the majority of our city council resolved to request the Provincial Government to so revise the city charter as to give them the power to make a city bylaw to punish newspaperboys for selling newspapers on Sunday.

Why stop at the newspaperboys? Why not punish other desecrators of the Sabbath?

Only last Sunday I saw and heard a dog barking at a crow, and a young fellow, evidently its owner, whistled as boldly as any good, well-thinking body would have done on a week day.

Surely, sir, if we are to continue to enjoy our boasted religious liberty, these desecrations of the Sabbath must be stopped.

PURITAN
Dec. 30, 1905

Those Opera House seats

Editor Province —

A lot of unfortunates asked me if I was familiar enough with the manager of the Opera House to approach him without undergoing any great risk of bodily injury with the suggestion regarding the handling of the large concourse which will undoubt-

— B.C. Archives A-07471

Arbutus Street in Kitsilano had a three-plank boardwalk, as this 1904 picture looking north shows. A reader asks why Vine St. could not have one.

Kitsilano and the Board of Works

Editor Province—

A number of the residents of Kitsilano feel rather sore over the way they have been treated by the Board of Works. Last June a petition was sent in to have Vine Street opened. It was referred to the City Engineer, and I presume the City Engineer is still working at it, for we have heard nothing more about it, but instead of opening up Vine Street, which would accommodate over 100 persons, the board went to work and laid a sidewalk out to the cannery, nearly a mile in length, for the accommodation of two residents out there and the Chinamen employed in the cannery.

Now, sir, I have no desire to rush into a controversy, but a number of us feel that we have been turned down, and we wish to know why.

If the representative of West Fairview would kindly tell us why a sidewalk was laid from Yew Street to the cannery, a distance of about a mile in length, while the residents of York Street and First, Second, Third and Fourth Avenues are dumped off the Kitsilano car into the mud and water to make their way as best they can through brush and over logs up Vine Street to the top of the hill, we would feel obliged.

Now, Mr. Editor, what we want is this: Open Vine Street to the top of the hill, as the terminus of the Street Railway is almost opposite Vine Street on the waterfront; or if finances will not permit this being done this fall, give us a three-plank walk to the top of the hill, a distance of three blocks, and we will wait until spring for the street. We ask no more, and we will be satisfied with no less.

Thanking you for your space, I remain
Yours truly

J. WHITE
Vancouver, Nov. 4, 1905

edly gather at the gallery doors on the evening of the 15th, 16th and 17th, but owing to the great financial loss undergone by the said gentleman, through the selling of season tickets (the cause of our woe) I deemed it safer to go at him through the press.

Would the said manager, therefore, deem it impertinent of me to suggest that the gallery throng be kept in line by policemen and not allowed to "bunch" as heretofore; the said "bunching" renders life unsafe and puts our gallantry too much to the test where ladies are the chief aggressors. To string them out along Granville Street would interfere with traffic, but they might be strung out to the back half a block, thence north up the lane to Georgia Street, thence west to the seaboard. In this way the last man in the line would run chances of seeing Faust by Saturday night anyway.

ONE OF THEM

Inadequate mail service

Editor Province —

Allow me to call attention to the wretchedly inadequate provision made for transporting the mail from Hartley Bay to Kitamaat.

The mail which left Vancouver Nov. 2 was so soaked with salt water while being taken from Hartley Bay to Kitamaat, that several of the letters were almost undecipherable, and the mail which left Hartley Bay Dec. 5 was delivered at Kitamaat, a distance of 40 miles away, on Dec. 18.

JOHN MONTAGUE
Hazelton, Jan. 6, 1906

Chilliwack and liquor

Editor Province —

Our attention has been called to a letter signed Boniface in your paper of Dec. 5, which makes the following statement: "Our neighbouring town of Chilliwack after years of drunken dry experience has recently gone wet in the interest of sobriety."

For sake of Boniface and those who profess to believe as he, we would like to say

Where were the young ladies?

Editor Province —

Vancouver was certainly en fête on Friday evening on the occasion of the hospital ball, and many were the opportunities for the votaries at the shrine of Terpsichore to display their talent.

The room at the hotel was a blaze of light and colour and the decorations were a standing compliment to the zealous and hardworking committee.

The floor was as perfect as it could possibly be under the circumstances, but the concrete substratum underneath rendered it somewhat hard and heavy going, and the absence of the pliable and bending spring floors so common in English ballrooms considerably handicapped the dancers, more particularly those whose years were betokened by their grey hairs and venerable bald heads, supplemented by a physical development that had lost its pristine youthful lissomeness.

One very notable feature was the surprising scarcity of the younger element, particularly among the ladies. By far the greater proportion of those present were buxom and matronly dames.

In order to make a thorough success of the charity ball, it is clearly evident that the magnetic influence of the "young girl" element be not excluded, as she gives to the dance that "go" which is so characteristic of English dances and which never fails to be popular and successful in consequence.

In England, it is customary to appoint an M.C. and committee. These gentlemen take particular caution that the dance "swings" well. They see that all strangers are sufficiently introduced, and it is a decided slight upon their attentiveness if there is a continual display of "wallflowers," especially when there are gentlemen waiting to be introduced.

ENGLISHMAN
Vancouver, Nov. 10, 1905

that Chilliwack did not go wet for the sake of sobriety, but Chilliwack went wet because it happened to have a population of over one thousand, and was an incorporated city, and so those seeking for licences could apply direct to the licence commissioners without petition; and more than this, these commissioners in direct opposition to the great majority of those who had a right to have a say in this matter, granted these licences, and the people could get no redress.

What has been our experience? Chilliwack the wet, in the short time of its existence, has had an increase of 100 per cent in convictions at its police court over the same length of time before the licenses were granted. And where previous to the granting of the licenses one policeman was all

that was found necessary to do the work, now we have two regularly paid policemen, and one special constable without salary.

Following close upon these licences has come the brothel, and even those who were at first in favour of the licences being granted do not want this, but it has come.

These are facts which ought to convince so fair a minded man as Boniface claims to be.

Signed on behalf of the Citizens' league.

H.G. STEWART, Secretary
Chilliwack, Dec. 30, 1905

1910 TO 1919

THE WAY WE WERE

— Vancouver Public Library, Special Collections 2599

Vancouver, circa 1912

Bundled up against the cold in an open Ford Model T Speedster, a woman drives herself and a companion. The steering wheel on the right side of the car serves as a reminder that B.C. drivers drove on the left side of the road until 1922.

In 1900, Thomas Plimley opened B.C.'s first car dealership in Victoria, and the first car he sold was an Oldsmobile with a four-horsepower engine. By 1916, there were close to 20 car dealers in the province.

WHILE EUROPE SMOULDERED

BY DAMIAN INWOOD

Despite clouds of war on the horizon, the decade starts optimistically.

The first Vancouver Exhibition in the summer of 1910 starts what will become a long tradition of summer fairs at Hastings Park.

In 1912, Vancouver's new pro hockey team, the Millionaires, beats its local rival, the New Westminster Royals, 8-3 in its first game.

The fuse has already been lit in the Balkans, a powderkeg which is set to explode in 1914 and launch the first global conflict.

Canada goes to war on Aug. 19, 1914, and the first 31,000 Canadian troops set sail for Europe on Oct. 3. By Armistice Day in 1918, more than 600,000 Canadians have slogged through the mud and rat-infested trenches.

The First World War dominates the decade as more than 60,000 Canadian soldiers die in the barbed-wire brutality of no man's land, the nightmare of mustard gas and the incessant shelling and sniper fire.

The "war to end all wars" leaves more than one million dead on the cratered battlefields of Europe.

The decade also includes the sinking of the *Titanic* on April 15, 1912, with 1,522 lives lost in the icy Atlantic.

Canadian Alexander Graham Bell's telephone speeds up communication with the first trans-Canada phone call.

Ireland explodes into violence during the Easter Rebellion as Dublin nationalists rise up and fight the British. It is a pattern that's doomed to repeat itself for the remainder of the century.

In Russia, ferment and revolution boil to the surface with the abdication and slaying of Czar Nicholas and his family.

In 1917, the Lenin-led Bolsheviks seize power, launching a socialist state that will lead to decades of communist rule.

In the same year the National Hockey League is born in Canada.

As First World War veterans come home to B.C. and are met by thousands of cheering citizens, the decade of doom draws to a close.

But change and discovery charge ahead as the first trans-Atlantic flight is made between Ireland and Newfoundland.

The age of commercial air travel has been heralded, and the globe has just become a little smaller.

> The "war to end all wars" leaves more than one million dead on the cratered battlefields of Europe

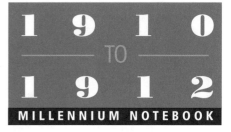

MILLENNIUM NOTEBOOK
1910 TO 1912

1910

May 6: Edward VII dies suddenly of pneumonia after ruling for nine years. His son, George V, becomes King.

Aug. 27: Thomas Edison unveils his latest U.S. invention, talking motion pictures. The "kinetophone" combines the sound of a phonograph with the images of a motion-picture camera.

Oct. 11: The first long-distance transmission sends power from the Niagara Falls generation plant to Berlin, now Kitchener, Ont. Toronto is being supplied by power from Niagara Falls by 1911.

1911

May 30: Driving a Marmon Wasp outfitted with the first rear-view mirror, Ray Harroun wins the first Indianapolis 500 auto race. He finishes in six hours, 42 minutes, eight seconds at an average speed of 120 kilometres per hour.

July 1: Polish biochemist Casimir Funk coins the name "vitamin" for chemicals necessary in the diet of animals and humans.

Oct. 9: Revolution breaks out in central China after a bomb explodes at the HQ of republican insurgents. Dr. Sun Yat Sen, Western-educated founder of the revolutionary movement, helps launch a republic, ending the 267-year-old Manchu dynasty.

Dec. 14: Norwegian explorer Roald Amundsen and four companions reach the South Pole, winning a race with Briton Robert F. Scott. Explorers have been to both ends of the globe in three years.

1912

April 15: An early report from Associated Press says the *Titanic,* stricken on its maiden voyage from Southampton, England, to New York—is afloat, "now in tow," and headed for Halifax, N.S.

As the tragic tale unfolds, a waiting world learns that more than 1,500 people have perished in the frigid Atlantic after the great ship's slide into the deep at 2:20 a.m. on

Canada goes to war

Canadian soldiers march off to war in 1914 as part of a young nation, inexperienced in the horrors of world conflict.

By the time the "war to end all wars" ends in 1918, they are veterans in ways of dying and Canada has come of age.

Of 619,000 Canadians who go overseas, 66,655 do not return and 179,000 are wounded.

Canada's finest hour comes at the capture of Vimy Ridge on April 9, 1917, changing the course of the First World War.

A massive artillery barrage is launched March 20 and by the time the infantry sets out, a million artillery shells have battered the Germans.

At 5:30 a.m. on April 9, 20,000 soldiers in four Canadian divisions advance.

The 4th Canadian Division's objective is Hill 145, the highest part of the Ridge and most heavily fortified, which is finally won on April 10.

Four soldiers win the Victoria Cross, the highest award for bravery. The action costs 3,598 Canadian lives.

Brigadier-General Alexander Ross, who commanded the 28th Battalion at Vimy, said: "It was Canada from the Atlantic to the Pacific on parade. I thought then . . . that I witnessed the birth of a nation."

April 15, 1912, two hours and 40 minutes after striking an iceberg.

Only 711 people, mostly women and children, are rescued by the Cunard liner *Carpathia* and brought to New York. The 42,000-tonne *Titanic*, then the largest, most luxurious ship in history, had enough lifeboats for less than half its 2,224 passengers and crew.

May 18: The first baseball strike takes place when 19 members of the Detroit Tigers refuse to play the Philadelphia Athletics. Tigers outfielder Ty Cobb is suspended after mauling a New York spectator who taunted him.

June 23: Niagara Falls bridge collapses and 47 die.

June 30: The worst tornado in Canadian history kills 65 and injures hundreds in Regina.

July: At the Fifth Olympiad in Stockholm, Jim Thorpe is the first person to win gold medals in both the decathlon and pentathlon. Thorpe, born in Oklahoma of Fox and Sac ancestry and a star halfback at the Indian School at Carlisle, Pa., receives his medals from King Gustav V of Sweden, who declares: "Sir, you are the greatest athlete in the world." Thorpe replies: "Thanks, King." He is later stripped of his medals for previously playing professional baseball and breaking the Olympic amateur rule.

Oct. 12: English journalist Thomas Wilby and American mechanic Jack Haney make the first cross-Canada car trip, driving 7,841 kilometres in a 1912 Reo from Halifax to Victoria in 52 days.

PASSAGES

MARK TWAIN
On April 21, 1910, the immensely popular Samuel Langhorne Clemens, better known as Mark Twain, dies at age 74 in Danbury, Conn. Twain's most famous work is *The Adventures of Tom Sawyer* (1876).

LEO TOLSTOY
Leo Tolstoy, author of *War and Peace,* has long been shunned by the Russian government but revered by the common folk. He dies on Nov. 20, 1910, at age 82.

PRODUCTS

'OLD JOE' CAMEL
Camel cigarettes are introduced by the R.J. Reynolds Co. in 1913. The package, which sells for a dime, features an image of a camel.

Lithographers base the picture on a photograph that a company photographer shot of a Barnum & Bailey circus camel named Old Joe.

The shot was taken with the animal in an unusual pose, with its nose held high, because Old Joe's trainer had just whacked him on the nose for misbehaving.

FILM

THE LITTLE TRAMP
Charlie Chaplin introduces his "little tramp" character to the world in 1914 in the one-reel Mack Sennett film, *Kid Auto Races at Venice.*

The character, an immediate hit, will be the protagonist in several of Chaplin's later full-length classics.

'BIRTH' OF AN INDUSTRY

D. W. Griffith's *Birth of a Nation,* a three-hour account of the U.S. Civil War and Reconstruction, includes such cinematic innovations as the close-up, the panoramic shot and the flashback. But the 1915 film reflects the racism of the time. Blacks are depicted as either foolish or evil. Despite its controversial thesis, the film is pivotal in the history of silent movies, taking the medium out of the nickelodeon and into that new phenomenon, the movie palace.

PASTIMES

'WITCH' BOARD

The Great War brings boom times for tea-leaf readers and crystal-ball gazers. The prognosticating Ouija board becomes a craze during wartime, when North Americans need a diversion—or a means to determine the fates of soldiers, their families and the nation. In 1967, at the height of the Vietnam War, Ouija board sales in the U.S. hit an all-time high of 2.3 million.

LEGENDS

LAWRENCE OF ARABIA

On Oct. 1, 1918, Lawrence of Arabia leads a triumphant Arab army into Damascus. Horsemen cavort in the streets as the greatest city in the Arab world celebrates its liberation from the yoke of the Ottoman Empire.

Major T. E. Lawrence—later played convincingly by Peter O'Toole in a 1962 movie—is a British adventurer, soldier and scholar.

After the outbreak of the First World War, he is attached to the intelligence section of the British army in Egypt.

He later writes about his Arabian adventures in *The Seven Pillars of Wisdom.*

Lawrence

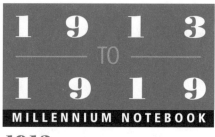

1913 TO 1919
MILLENNIUM NOTEBOOK

1913

June 4: Stepping up their efforts to win the vote, English suffragettes take to smashing windows and throwing firebombs. On Derby Day at Epsom Downs, Emily Wilding Davison runs on to the racetrack in front of King George V's prize horse and tries to seize the reins. She is trampled and dies four days later. Her death galvanizes the movement.

Aug. 6: Canada's first air fatality occurs in Victoria when U.S. barnstormer John Bryant dies in the crash of his Curtiss seaplane.

Oct. 10: U.S. President Woodrow Wilson pushes a button in Washington to detonate eight tons of dynamite, opening the last segment of the Panama Canal. Nicknamed "The Big Ditch," it officially opens for business on April 15, 1914. The United States spent $352 million US on the canal, which needed 200 million cubic metres in excavation. Thousands of construction workers lost their lives.

1914

May 14: Oil is found in the Turner Valley, south of Calgary, sparking Canada's first oil boom.

May 28: The Canadian Pacific ocean liner *Empress of Ireland* collides with the Norwegian ship *Storstad* in the St. Lawrence River, sinking in less than 15 minutes. In what is the world's eighth largest marine disaster, 1,024 die.

June 12: The Boy Scout Association of Canada is incorporated.

June 19: A dust explosion in the Hillcrest, Alta., mine kills 189 in Canada's worst mine disaster.

War is brewing in Europe. The major powers are lurching toward a global conflict that will bring about the collapse of empires and a realignment of world power. On one side is the Triple Entente, comprising Britain, France and Russia; the alliance will eventually include Serbia, Belgium, Italy and Japan. On the other is a coalition called the Central Powers: Germany, the Austro-Hungarian Empire, the Ottoman Empire and Bulgaria.

June 28: The flash point comes when Austria's Archduke Franz Ferdinand and his wife, Sophie von Hohenberg, are shot to death in Sarajevo, capital of the Austro-Hungarian province of Bosnia-Herzegovina. Their assassination by a Serbian nationalist prompts Austria-Hungary's attack on Serbia and launches the war.

Aug. 19: Canada formally declares war on Germany and Austria-Hungary, 16 days after Britain's entry into the war.

Oct. 3: About 31,000 Canadian volunteer troops sail for Europe.

1915

Jan. 25: Canadian Alexander Graham Bell in New York and assistant Thomas Watson in San Francisco pick up telephones and begin the first transcontinental conversation. The telephone's inventor makes the connection and says: "Hoy, hoy, Mr. Watson, are you there? Do you hear me?" Watson responds: "Yes, Mr. Bell, I hear you perfectly. Do you hear me well?"

April 12: Germany uses chlorine gas bombs and shells at Ypres, opening a four-mile gap in the allied lines. On May 3, John McCrae of Ontario writes the poem "In Flanders Field" at Ypres. It is published in England's *Punch* magazine in December.

May 8: The *Lusitania* is sunk by two German torpedoes off the coast of Ireland with 1,251 passengers and 650 crew aboard; 1,195 lives are lost.

1916

Jan. 28: Canadian women are first granted the right to vote and hold political office in Manitoba.

April 24: Rebellion erupts in Ireland in what becomes known as the Easter Rising of armed Irish insurgents. About 2,000 rebels in Dublin rise against the British and police arrest the leaders and declare martial law. At least 450 people are killed and more than 2,500 wounded, mostly civilians. The fierce but short-lived rebellion has little public support. People hiss the rebel leaders, but the insurgents become martyrs when they are convicted of treason and hanged Aug. 3. The Irish Free State achieves dominion status, with self-government, in 1922.

June 13: Emily Murphy, an Edmonton magistrate, is the first woman to become a lower court judge in the British Empire.

1917

March 16: Russia's Czar Nicholas II abdicates, saying: "May God help Russia." Lenin returns from exile four days later.

April 4: Women get the vote in B.C.

June 2: Canadian air ace William Avery (Billy) Bishop is awarded the Victoria Cross for a single-handed attack on a German airfield. He eventually shoots down 72 enemy aircraft.

June 7: The first women elected to a provincial legislature are Louise McKinney and Roberta MacAdams in Alberta.

July 25: The Income Tax War Bill, Canada's first national income tax, is introduced as a temporary measure.

Billy Bishop shot down 72 enemy planes

Oct. 15: A Dutch-Javanese courtesan and exotic dancer known as Mata Hari, or "Eye of the Morning," is executed by a firing squad in Paris. Mata Hari, born Margarethe Geertruida Zelle, had been convicted of spying for the Germans.

Nov. 2: The Balfour Declaration, saying Britain favours "the establishment in Palestine of a national home for the Jewish people," is issued by foreign secretary Arthur Balfour. British troops seize Palestine from the Ottoman Turks.

Mata Hari

Nov. 6: Bolsheviks capture Russian government buildings and the Winter Palace in what's later called the October Revolution.

Nov. 26: The National Hockey League is formed with the four original teams: Montreal Canadiens, Montreal Wanderers, Ottawa Senators and Toronto Arenas.

1918

Jan. 23: An explosion in the Allan Shaft mine, Nova Scotia, kills 88 men.

March 16: The districts of Mackenzie, Keewatin and Franklin are created in the Northwest Territories and officially brought into the Dominion of Canada in 1920.

— National Archives

The scene in Halifax harbour looking south after the explosion of a munitions ship in 1917.

Munitions blast devastates Halifax

On Dec. 6, 1917, much of Halifax, Nova Scotia, is destroyed by an explosion that levels 325 acres, kills 2,000 people and injures 9,000. A Norwegian relief ship laden with supplies for war-torn Europe plows into the French munitions ship *Mont Blanc,* loaded with 4,000 tons of TNT and a cocktail of explosives.

The day dawns bright and clear in Halifax, but at 9:05 a.m. the bustling harbour is transformed into a nightmare scene.

The crew of the *Mont Blanc* takes to lifeboats, screaming warnings.

The explosion comes 20 minutes after the collision, enough time for spectators, including many children, to run to the waterfront to watch the burning ship.

A blinding white flash triggers the biggest man-made explosion prior to the age of nuclear weapons.

March 18: Daylight Savings Time is first implemented in Canada to increase war production.

March: Soldiers start falling ill at Fort Riley in Kansas as the Spanish Flu pandemic starts its deadly sweep around the world. At least 20 million people die.

April 21: The Red Baron, Manfred von Richthofen, is shot down and killed at the Battle of the Somme. English fighter pilot Edward Mannock says, "I hope he roasted all the way down."

July 17: Just after midnight, deposed Russian Czar Nicholas II, Czarina Alexandra, their son Alexis, and their four daughters, Olga, Tatiana, Marie and Anastasia, are shot to death by the Bolsheviks.

Nov. 11: An armistice is signed to end the First World War in which an estimated 10 million soldiers were killed. In 1931, Nov. 11 is renamed Remembrance Day and declared a legal holiday.

1919

Jan. 1: Federal law now permanently allows women to vote.

Feb. 17: Sir Wilfrid Laurier dies in Ottawa.

March 29: Robert Goddard, a Worcester, Mass. physics professor, publishes a monograph called *A Method of Reaching Extreme Altitudes,* saying a trip to the moon by rocket may some day be possible. Newspapers ridicule Goddard's prediction.

May 15: The Winnipeg General Strike begins when 30,000 workers from 52 unions walk off the job to support metalworkers and building-trades workers who had struck on May 1. Strike leaders are jailed. On "Bloody Saturday," June 21, armed and mounted police charge demonstrators, killing two and wounding 20. The strike is called off on June 25.

June 6: The Canadian National Railway is incorporated, becoming the longest railway system in North America, with more than 50,000 kilometres of track.

June 15: Capt. John Alcock of Great Britain and Lt. Arthur Brown of the U.S. make the first non-stop trans-Atlantic flight from Newfoundland to Ireland in a Vickers-Vimy biplane.

They complete the 3,000 kilometres in 16 hours, 12 minutes, at an average speed of 195 km/h.

VANCOUVER ISLAND, 1912 Women enjoy a game of tug-of-war as their gentlemen friends look on with amusement at Sooke River flats on Vancouver Island. At the time, simple-to-use box cameras and others using roll film were becoming more popular. Although the resulting pictures, like this one, were less sharp, they were also more candid than the posed shots previously taken with view cameras.

— B.C. Archives D-08051

1910

A Bowen Island dynamite plant explodes on March 12, killing five. The blast is felt in Nanaimo.

The provincial government purchases the Songhees Indian Reserve, which makes up 115 acres of downtown Victoria. The band's 43 families receive $10,000 each.

A crowd of 3,500 in Minoru Park, Richmond, watches the first airplane flight west of Winnipeg. The aircraft, a Curtiss pusher biplane, is piloted by Charles K. Hamilton.

On April 20, a man in Surrey is fined $10 for speeding. His 1907 Marion automobile was caught going 12 m.p.h.

The B.C. government boasts an $8 million surplus.

1911

Thieves get away with $250,000 from a New Westminster bank—the greatest bank vault robbery in North American history.

A census records the population of B.C. at 392,480.

The Vancouver Golf Club, with a nine-hole course, opens in Coquitlam. The old Austin farm house is used as a clubhouse and includes a dormitory for golfers who miss the last tram back to their city homes.

Japanese settlers begin growing strawberries in Surrey, and the nearby community hall comes to be known as Strawberry Hill.

1912

The first passenger flight in B.C. is piloted by Billy Stark with *Province* reporter James Hewitt strapped to the lower wing. The eight-minute flight travels 10 kilometres at a speed of 65 kilometres per hour.

The Vancouver Millionaires, wearing white and maroon sweaters, defeat the New Westminster Royals 8-3 in their first pro hockey game.

1913

In August, coal mine strikers take over Nanaimo and riot against Japanese and Chinese workers hired to break the strike. Attorney General Bowser calls in 1,000 troops to bring the situation under control.

Poet Pauline Johnson dies. Her ashes are buried in Stanley Park.

— B.C. Archives F-08990

EAST KOOTENAY, 1914 A Kootenay chief and his family pose in traditional dress.

Opposite: **RICHMOND, 1918** A woman and her son watch a house burn to the ground during a spring fire in Steveston. The Chinese and Japanese sections of Moncton Street were razed, leaving 600 homeless, and most of the business district, including three canneries and three hotels, was destroyed.

— Richmond City Archives 1977-11-12

— B.C. Archives E-04017

Indian Potlatch
Duncan, BC.

COWICHAN, CIRCA 1911 Although banned by the federal government in 1884, potlatches remained an integral part of Cowichan life

1914

Militia groups in the Lower Mainland begin receiving mobilization orders for the First World War on Aug. 10. By Aug. 26, the first regiments leave Vancouver.

Myrtle and Alex Philip open the Rainbow Lodge in Whistler, soon to be a popular summer resort. Myrtle ran a general store for more than 30 years and Alex wrote romance novels.

1915

The first trans-Canada phone call is placed between Vancouver and Montreal.

The Vancouver Millionaires defeat the Ottawa Senators for the Stanley Cup.

After the *Lusitania* is sunk, a mob of anti-German rioters trashes a German-owned beer garden and brewery in Victoria.

A Howe Sound mining accident kills 56.

Originally founded in 1908 as a branch of McGill University, the University of B.C. becomes an independent university on Sept. 30 and now has 379 students.

1916

The Workman's Compensation Act is passed into law. It is considered the most advanced legislation of its kind.

1917

On April 5, B.C. women win the right to vote and hold provincial office.

Prohibition becomes law on Oct. 1.

1918

Albert (Ginger) Goodwin, a socialist labour leader, is shot to death. There are two versions of his death. Unionists believe provincial police hired cop Dan Campbell to kill Goodwin. Campbell, however, swears in court that Goodwin was armed, and that he fired to save his own life.

On Oct. 26, the *Princess Sophia* steamship sinks in Lynn Canal, 50 kilometres northwest of Juneau, Alaska. All 343 passengers and crew die, making it the worst shipping accident in B.C. history.

1919

Fourteen hundred veterans return to Vancouver aboard the *Empress of Asia*. They are greeted by 40,000 citizens.

—Melissa Radler

— B.C. Archives F-06223

— Vancouver City Archives MIL P90 N156

VANCOUVER, 1918 The First World War, the "war to end all wars," ended Nov. 11, 1918. After the general public was alerted with factory whistles, Vancouver residents organized an immediate victory procession. Beaming with pride, veterans Col. Alfred Markham, Major "Reggie" Tupper, R.S.M. James Robinson, Major C.C. Owen and Crimean War veteran J.R. Grant march down Granville Street, near Georgia.

— Vancouver Public Library, Special Collections 13212

Opposite: **ROGERS PASS, 1910** On March 5, the worst avalanche disaster in B.C. history buried a 63-man clean-up crew working along this stretch of the Canadian Pacific Railway. Just hours before this picture was taken, the men set out near Rogers Pass to clear snow from the tracks. Without warning, the avalanche struck, killing all but one man.

VANCOUVER, 1916 Six female gas-station attendants pose in front of the Imperial Oil service station at Broadway and Granville. With Vancouver's men fighting the First World War in Europe, women were permitted to take over jobs previously considered unladylike.

CHILLIWACK, 1912 The Jesperson family pose with a giant haypile on their Chilliwack farm. In 1884, Henry Jesperson and his wife, Andrea, emigrated from Denmark to B.C., where they bought 240 acres of land covered with dense brush. Using axes, brush hooks, saws and oxen, the couple cleared the land, planted crops, and had eight children.

— Vancouver Public Library, Special Collections 6232

VANCOUVER, 1914 For two months, 376 mostly Sikh migrants aboard the *Komagata Maru* languished in Burrard Inlet, awaiting permission to enter Canada. At the time, Indians were kept out of Canada by a law that required them to come directly from India in one continuous trip, a service that wasn't provided at the time. That was why the migrants had chartered this Japanese-owned freighter in Hong Kong, but on July 23 officials ordered the ship to leave Canadian waters.

— Chilliwack Museum and Archives P2279

SUNSHINE COAST, CIRCA 1913 Fred Klein (far left), a friend, and George Klein pose at Kleindale (Pender Harbour), where they cut the trees that were used to build Lumberman's Arch in Stanley Park. In 1912 the Klein brothers founded a 30-man logging camp at this spot on the Sunshine Coast, clearing the land and draining its salt marshes before settling permanently in the area. This picture was submitted by *Province* reader Lorna Klein.

VANCOUVER, 1914 Getting there is half the battle … Electric Railway's poster child for a public safety no-no is this 1914 tram, roaming the streets of Vancouver at 300 per cent capacity.

— Coast Mountain Bus Company Ltd.

— Vancouver Fire Department Archives

These firefighters took a blow in 1915 when Vancouver city council solved a budgetary problem by cutting all police and fire department salaries by 20 per cent. The city's action was widely criticized and prompted letters such as the one below.

Civic salary reductions

Editor Province —

It has always seemed to me unjust that, because the council had under its thumb one body of men who cannot escape, that particular section of the community should be compelled to bear a burden which is by every fair thinking man admitted to be a necessary burden but one for which every citizen is equally liable. The question of remitting it in the case of the firemen and police is under consideration.

Let it be borne in mind that the finance committee spent much time setting the salaries on a basis that they judged right and that the war has not made it any cheaper to live and it will be seen that it is as hard for one set of employees as another.

I suggest that the mayor get in touch with the Board of Trade and try to get it arranged that every man employed in the city be asked to agree to give, if married, two per cent of his salary, and if unmarried, four per cent. In this way I do not think anyone would kick and the city would get very much more for its employment scheme. The present scheme of robbing one class of men of 20 per cent is nothing short of iniquitous. No one receiving less than $60 a month should be asked to contribute.

E. Gilman, Feb. 15, 1915

That early morning whistle

Editor Province—

"Just Grandma" evidently forgets that in those numerous hospitals Vancouver is favoured with there are hundreds of patients lying, perhaps tossing, the long, weary night through. Grandpas, as well as grandmas, younger people, as well as little children and babies, nervous and suffering pain, weary through exhaustion, fall into a sweet calm sleep to the dawn of day.

Are they not to be considered? Saying nothing about the faithful nurses, creeping through those long corridors on tip toe, all to give their suffering charges the quiet calm they are so much in need of.

Again, must the 150,000 citizens, more or less, all be disturbed unnecessarily by that 6 a.m. whistle, many of them unquestionably weary with business anxieties during these strenuous times? Are they, too, not entitled to their morning nap? There seems little excuse for those men not to get to their work on time without the whistle.

Just Another Grandma
April 5, 1915

Privilege of women voters

Editor Province —

In view of the civic elections which are again to engage the attention of the electors of the city, will you please publish the following letter? Having attended a meeting held by the Woman's Forum in the latter part of January, held for the help and possible instruction of the women voters of our city, would it be in order for one to offer a few suggestions to the Woman's Forum?

As we are demanding equal rights with men in all things, why not live up to what we are demanding? That meeting, as was generally understood, was called for the sole purpose of giving the women voters the privilege of hearing the mayoralty candidates and other men running for public office discuss their different platforms, in order that these women voters might have an intelligent idea of the relative merits of the different candidates.

Unfortunately our city faces the necessity of holding a second election within the space of a few weeks. Would it not be well for the Woman's Forum to continue their educational efforts by public meetings where women would be allowed to ask questions, which should receive proper consideration and answers?

At the late meeting questions for further enlightenment were discouraged and the educational value of the meeting was largely lost. At meetings for men, proper questions from the audience receive proper answers. It will be absolutely necessary to accord the same treatment to women if we hope to reach the object of our ambition and be able to fulfill the rights we are demanding.

I would respectfully suggest to all women ratepayers of our city that they take more active interest in civic matters. All women voters should take note, and act accordingly, as to what class and what kind of men are running for civic office. It is such an important matter. Indiscriminate voting is to be deplored.

(Mrs.) Jean J. Forster
537 Richards Street,
March 15, 1915

Flour and sugar increases

Editor Province—

I am sure that many people in Vancouver would like to know what has caused the increase in the price of flour and sugar. I understand that the bakeries pay no more for flour than they did before the rise, and bread is still the same price, five cents a loaf.

What is the cause of the increased prices? Someone should explain. I am sure the public would like to know. Has the city council no interest in this question that so vitally affects the people who elected the aldermen? All the talk about the full dinner pail is not worth the time it took to tell of it. The idea of the city trying to raise more money on the strength of the taxes is simply outrageous. How are the "taxes," now due, going to be paid?—much less the 1915 taxes. Out of the revenue from the empty houses, or from the greatly reduced rents of those occupied? I think these questions are of sufficient importance to be explained.

Corntassel
Feb. 19, 1915

Horseshoeing costs

Editor Province —

As an old subscriber and a businessman in this city for a number of years would you kindly allow me to protest most emphatically against the statement made before the Board of Works recently by some horse authority that any horseshoer would undertake to contract to shoe city horses for $19 per year. Such a statement is misleading and would tend to do grave injury to members of our business in this city by giving our customers an altogether erroneous idea of prices and profits of our trade. As a horseshoer of long and wide experience I have no hesitation in making the assertion that it could not possibly be done at a profit, for the material, wages and other expense incidental to running a business of this sort would eat up the whole $19.

The utter absurdity of this remarkably clever and economical horseshoeing authority is quite apparent when he states that nine dollars worth of shoes are thrown away per horse per annum. I would like to ask him what do the shoes cost for a heavy horse per year supposing the horse is shod once a month as every working horse should be in order to protect and give the proper care and attention necessary to the feet. Then there are horses which require very careful and skillful shoeing and such additions to ordinary work as leather pads, rubber pads, bar shoes and so forth which is bound to raise the average price. I consider the statement of that individual erroneous and that the city is getting its horses shod at a very fair and reasonable price.

John G. Alexander
Feb. 19, 1915

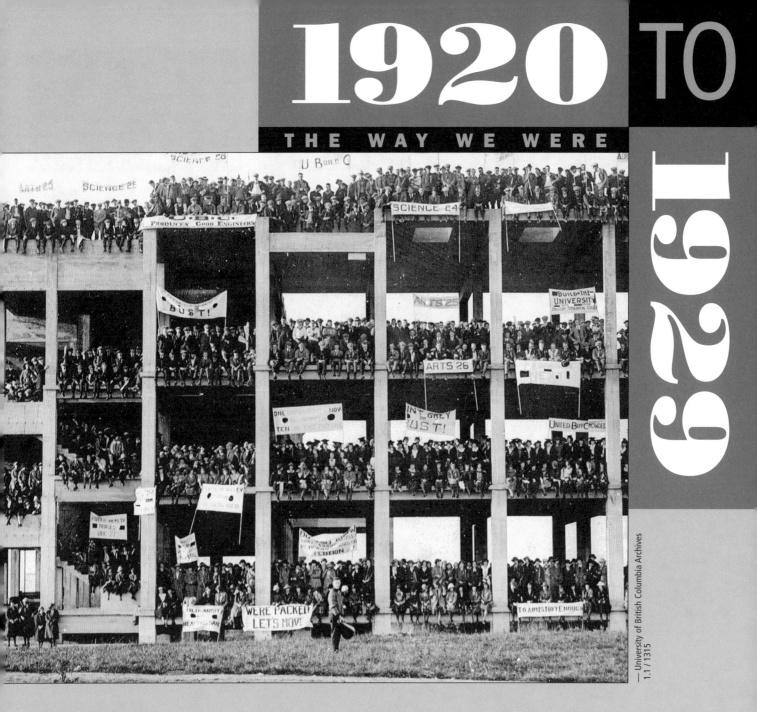

— University of British Columbia Archives 1.1 / 1315

Vancouver, 1922

Student demos are nothing new to Vancouver. To pressure the government into finishing work on the Point Grey campus of the University of B.C., students end Varsity Week with a "Great Trek." They take their class banners and climb the skeleton of the science building at Point Grey. Work has been stalled on the new campus since the outbreak of the First World War, with students forced to live in crowded tents and rundown shacks on the grounds of Vancouver General Hospital. The students' campaign succeeds and the university moves to the new campus in 1925.

RUSHING TOWARD A CRASH

By Damian Inwood

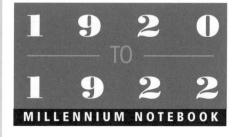

he Roaring Twenties come in dry but soon go wet as B.C. repeals its prohibition laws.

A 1920 referendum, citizens vote in favour of demon drink being allowed in the province.

It doesn't come a moment too soon.

The previous December, W.C. Findlay, B.C.'s prohibition commissioner and administrator, has been nabbed in Blaine for illegally importing carloads of whiskey.

By April 1921, the laws have been changed and government liquor stores are open for business.

That same June, Canada's post First World War population is almost 8.8 million, with B.C. boasting 524,582 people.

The burgeoning car industry has to make an adjustment on Jan. 1, 1922. That's when B.C. drivers switch from driving British-style, on the left, to driving on the right side of the road.

In the spring of 1922, 12,000 coal miners go on strike in B.C. and Alberta. The strike drags on until August.

That same year comes an invention that will revolutionize the way Canadians get around in winter.

A 15-year-old Quebec inventor,

Joseph-Armand Bombardier, test-drives the first snowmobile.

It is built using four runners from a horse-drawn sleigh, powered by a motor-driven wooden propeller.

Bombardier's first run down the streets of Valcourt causes a sensation, as his noisy contraption sends horses bolting and is chased by barking dogs.

In 1926, a Scottish inventor unveils a new device that some will praise and others curse. He is John Logie Baird, who demonstrates the transmission of moving pictures on a cathode ray tube, which he calls "television."

The next year, the first "talkie" features Al Jolson in *The Jazz Singer.*

In 1929, the first quick-frozen fish fillets are developed by Archibald Huntsman in Halifax and introduced in Toronto.

The world economy is about to go into a deep freeze as well. Oct. 24, known as Black Thursday, sees share prices take a downward elevator ride on Wall Street.

The following Tuesday is even worse and, as panic selling sets in, some investors commit suicide.

It's the darkness before the dawn of the Dirty Thirties and the Great Depression.

> A 1920 referendum votes in favour of demon drink being allowed in the province

1920

Jan. 10: Canada becomes a founding member of the League of Nations in Geneva. Set up under the Treaty of Versailles at the end of the First World War, the league fails to prevent the Second World War and is replaced by the United Nations in 1945.

Feb. 1: The Royal North-West Mounted Police joins the Dominion Police to become the Royal Canadian Mounted Police, headquartered in Regina.

Feb. 24: Unhappy, alienated veterans have formed the German Workers Party in Munich. They release a list of goals and programs attacking Jews, large property owners and capitalists. Propaganda chief is Adolf Hitler.

May 7: The Group of Seven painters exhibit 100 paintings at the Art Gallery of Toronto. The Canadian landscapes get positive reviews but are not popular with the public. Only three are sold.

Dec. 14: The British parliament divides Ireland in two. The northern territory will be the scene of violence between the Catholic minority and Protestant majority for the rest of the century.

1921

Feb. 18: The first gyroplane, or helicopter, the brainchild of Etienne Oehmichan, a French designer, successfully takes off in Paris.

March 26: The *Bluenose* schooner is launched at Lunenburg, N.S., and goes on to be undefeated as winner of the International Fisherman's Trophy for fastest sailing vessel in the North Atlantic fishing fleet.

July 27: Frederick Banting and Charles Best identify insulin, the lack of which results in diabetes, at the University of Toronto. They get the Nobel Prize in 1923.

Sept. 7: In a bid to keep tourists in Atlantic City past Labour Day, the chamber of commerce stages a "Fall Frolic." Newspapers ask readers to send in photographs of

Booze was illegal—and lucrative

The war against evil booze is waning in Canada just as Prohibition is gaining momentum in the U.S.

In 1921, after four dry years, B.C. allows alcohol to be sold under government control.

It is just as well, as speakeasies and "blind pigs" have been popping up everywhere.

Doctors have seen long lineups outside their offices from epidemics of "ill" people seeking prescriptions for drugstore booze, especially at Christmas time.

A Prohibition-era photograph of a Toronto tippler being arrested.

— National Archives

South of the border, it's a different story as a country hooked on jazz and flappers seeks to slake its thirst, despite strict laws forbidding alcohol.

U.S. Prohibition means a bonanza for Canadian smugglers intent on rum-running across the line.

Violent crime-gang battles sprout along borders and coastlines.

Newspaper cartoons feature leaky maps of Canada with Uncle Sam attempting to stem the alcoholic tide from the north.

Quebec is actually first out of the gate, beating B.C. by a year and legalizing alcohol sales in 1919.

Even in the Bible belt of the Canadian Prairies, the laws are relaxed during the Roaring '20s.

Manitoba sets up government liquor stores in 1923, followed by Alberta and Saskatchewan in 1924, Newfoundland in 1925, Ontario and New Brunswick in 1927 and Nova Scotia in 1930. The last bastion of Canadian Prohibition, Prince Edward Island, will hang on to the "noble experiment" until 1948.

---

beautiful women and the winners take part in a beauty contest. Margaret Gorman, a petite 16-year-old from Washington, D.C., is crowned the first Miss America.

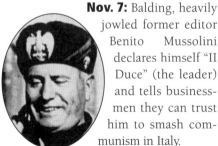

Mussolini

Nov. 7: Balding, heavily jowled former editor Benito Mussolini declares himself "Il Duce" (the leader) and tells businessmen they can trust him to smash communism in Italy.

Nov. 21: The maple leaf is Canada's official emblem, after King George V's authorization.

Dec. 6: Agnes Campbell Macphail is the first woman elected to the House of Commons.

1922

Feb. 25: Henri-Desire Landru, the so-called modern Bluebeard, is guillotined in Versailles, France, for the murders of 10 women and a young boy.

April 3: Josef Stalin is elected general secretary of the Central Committee of the Russian Communist Party.

June 14: In a silent march in Washington, blacks from every state show their support for a bill to make lynching a federal crime. The measure passes in the House but fails in the Senate. There are 57 reported lynchings in 1922.

Nov. 5: After six years of fruitless digging in Egypt's Valley of the Kings, British archaeologist Howard Carter discovers "a magnificent tomb with seals intact." The contents of the tomb of the boy pharaoh Tutankhamen include a coffin of solid gold with a painted likeness of King Tut.

JOURNALISM

MAGAZINES DEBUT

Henry Luce and Briton Hadden, classmates at Hotchkiss and Yale, establish an institution of American journalism on March 3, 1923, with publication of the first issue of *Time* magazine. It compresses the week's happenings in the world into 28 pages, minus six pages of advertising sold at giveaway rates.

Reader's Digest makes its debut in February 1922 in New York with articles "of lasting interest" condensed from books and other magazines into a pocket-size monthly.

PRODUCTS

CHANEL NO. 5

In 1922, Coco Chanel introduces Chanel No. 5, which will become the world's best-known perfume. The French-born couturier launches the movement toward simplicity, practicality and unfussy elegance in women's clothing.

CRAZES

CROSSWORD PUZZLES

Crossword mania sweeps North America in April 1924 after a new publishing company owned by Richard Simon and M. Lincoln Schuster puts out the first book of crosswords.

MAH-JONG

W. A. Hammond, a San Francisco lumber merchant, imports thousands of sets of mah-jong, a Chinese tile game, in 1922.

It soon becomes a craze.

The wealthy buy $500 sets, the Mah-jong League of America is formed, and many a dinner party ends with guests setting up ivory and bamboo tiles on green tables.

PASSAGES

HARRY HOUDINI

The world-famous magician and escape artist dies Oct. 31, 1926, in Detroit, at age 52 of peritonitis. It's said that a few days before, he had been injured by a McGill University student in Montreal who wanted to test Houdini's claim that he could withstand any body blow but hit him in the abdomen before he was ready.

LIZZY BORDEN

The woman accused and then acquitted of killing her father and stepmother with an axe in 1892 dies as a recluse June 2, 1927, at the age of 69.

PRODUCTS

THE LA-Z-BOY

While tinkering with pieces of plywood and a yardstick in 1928, Edwin Shoemaker and cousin Edward Knabusch fashion an austere, wood-slat reclining lawn chair as a new product for their Floral City Furniture Co. in Monroe, Mich. The "La-Z-Boy" will become one of the best-known names in furniture.

MEDICINE

PENICILLIN, A MAGIC BULLET

Scottish physician Alexander Fleming is intrigued by the observation that most soldiers with war wounds die of infection rather than the wounds. His research at St. Mary's Hospital Medical School in London focuses on how to kill the deadly bacteria.

Penicillin, his landmark discovery, which he reports without fanfare in September 1928, will become the wonder antibiotic of the Second World War.

OMENS

SEEDS OF THE HOLOCAUST

In 1925, Adolf Hitler publishes the first volume of *Mein Kampf* (My Struggle), an attempt to give an intellectual basis to his leadership of the Nazi Party. The book contains little original thought but synthesizes ideas that prove to be incendiary in unstable postwar Germany. The racially superior German people, Hitler writes, are threatened by liberalism, Marxism and Bolshevism, all of which are manipulated behind the scenes by the Jews.

1 9 2 3 TO 1 9 2 9
MILLENNIUM NOTEBOOK

1923

Feb. 17: A young black woman named Bessie Smith records "T'ain't Nobody's Bizness If I Do" and "Down-Hearted Blues", introducing North America to a new kind of music called "the blues." The record sells two million copies within a year.

April 21: Dance marathons are all the rage. Magdalene Wolfe of Cleveland sets a world record by holding the dance floor for 73 hours. Four months later, Kalamazoo, Mich., passes an ordinance banning dancing couples from gazing into each other's eyes.

Sept. 1: An earthquake and fire ravage Tokyo and Yokohama. At least 91,000 people are thought to have been killed .

1924

Jan. 21: Vladimir Ilyich Lenin dies at age 54. Lenin, the first Communist head of state and mastermind of the Russian Revolution, lays the groundwork for a dictatorship later to be perfected by a former seminary student turned political thug, Josef Stalin.

Jan. 26: The Canadian Red Ensign becomes the official flag.

A PERFECTLY DEVELOPED MAN

Scrawny Italian immigrant Angelo Siciliano, tired of getting beaten up by bullies in New York City, decides to transform himself. As a teenager, Siciliano develops his "dynamic tension" fitness method and in 1922, aged 29, he wins the "most perfectly developed man" contest at Madison Square Garden.

Siciliano changes his name to Charles Atlas, teams up with an advertising executive and soon is selling mail-order fitness programs to teenagers across North America.

April 1: The Royal Canadian Air Force is created.

1925

March 21: Tennessee Gov. Austin Peay bans teaching the theory of evolution in schools. The American Civil Liberties Union offers to defend any teacher willing to test the law. John Thomas Scopes, a biology teacher, takes up the call. The "Scopes Monkey Trial" begins July 10 with lawyer Clarence Darrow leading the defence. The prosecutor is William Jennings Bryan, who stands by the literal interpretation of the Bible. Scopes is found guilty and fined $100 on July 21.

March 30: The last non-NHL team to win the Stanley Cup is the Victoria Cougars of the Western Canada Hockey League. The Cougars beat the Montreal Canadiens by three games to one.

June 10: The United Church of Canada forms from a union of Methodists, Presbyterians and Congregationalists.

Nov. 31: RCA Victor makes the first electronic sound recording at the New York Metropolitan Opera House.

1926

Jan. 27: Scottish inventor John Logie Baird demonstrates the wireless transmission of moving pictures on a cathode ray tube. He calls it "television."

March 16: Robert H. Goddard, a 43-year-old Massachussetts university physics instructor, meets with two assistants on a frozen farm field and detonates the world's first liquid-fuel (oxygen and gasoline) rocket. It flies 184 feet and reaches an altitude of 41 feet and a top speed of 103 km/h before landing in a cabbage patch.

April 26: Mae West is arrested in New York City for performing in the play *Sex*, in which she stars as a prostitute. The Society for the Suppression of Vice persuades police to close the show.

Sept. 25: Ford Motor Co. in Detroit begins a 40-hour, five-day work week. Pay is $6 a day.

Dec. 5: Mystery novelist Agatha Christie disappears from her home in Sunningdale, England. She is found at a health-spa hotel, 11 days later, joining guests in games and conversation but suffering from amnesia.

The crash of 1929

The reckless optimism of the Jazz Age fuels a decade of spectacular gains on Wall Street. But the autumn of 1929 brings omens of calamity. There are hints of a worldwide economic slowdown and warnings from experts that stocks are grossly overpriced. Stock prices peak in early September, then weaken. On Oct. 24, panic sets in. Stock prices slide in a rush to sell. Bankers step in and stabilize the market, but not before nearly 13 million shares change hands on Black Thursday.

It should have been called Grey Thursday, for the following Tuesday, Oct. 29, is one of the most devastating days in economic history. The next day is nearly as bad. Some investors commit suicide. Did The Crash cause the Great Depression that followed? Nearly 70 years later, no one really knows.

— New York Daily News

Brokers and investors mill about on Wall Street in the confusion that prevailed during the stock market crash of 1929.

Dec. 25: In Japan, an era ends with the death of the 47-year-old Emperor Yoshihito. He is succeeded by his son, Hirohito.

1927

Jan. 7: A black basketball team organized by Chicago businessman Abe Saperstein plays its first game in Hinckley, Ill., before a crowd of 300 for a payout of $75. Called the Savoy Big Five, the team sets out on the road in a Model T Ford and becomes known as the Harlem Globetrotters.

Jan. 9: A fire at the overcrowded Laurier Place Theatre in Montreal kills 76 people.

May 19: *Wings,* a silent World War I epic filmed in San Antonio, Texas, makes its premiere. The next year, *Wings* will be the first film to win an Academy Award for best picture.

May 20: Charles Lindbergh becomes the first person to make a solo crossing of the Atlantic by airplane, taking 33 hours to fly from Long Island to Paris.

July 1: The Diamond Jubilee of Canadian Confederation is celebrated with the first coast-to-coast radio network broadcast of Parliament Hill celebrations.

Sept. 30: Babe Ruth hits his 60th home run of the season against the Washington Senators at Yankee Stadium. Ruth's record will stand until another Yankee, Roger Maris, hits 61 in 1961, a record surpassed by Mark McGwire's 70 home runs in 1998.

Oct. 6: *The Jazz Singer* is the first "talkie." The first spoken words in a feature film are those of Al Jolson, who says, "Wait a minute, wait a minute. You ain't heard nothin' yet." Crowds jump to their feet and applaud.

1928

Nov. 18: A mischievous mouse named Mickey is introduced to the world in the animated cartoon *Steamboat Willie.* Mickey Mouse is the brainchild of a 26-year-old illustrator named Walter Elias Disney and his wife, Lillian. The inspiration comes from field mice that wandered into Disney's studio in Kansas City when he was producing advertising films. The mouse will become the symbol of Disney's entertainment empire.

1929

Feb. 14: The nondescript S.M.C. Cartage Co. building in Chicago gains instant fame. Inside are seven bloody bodies and a gangland mystery. It is thought the execution-style murders result from a liquor-smuggling war between Al (S c a r f a c e) Capone and George (Bugs) Moran. No one is ever charged in the St. Valentine's Day Massacre.

May 16: Douglas Fairbanks presents the first Academy Awards to actor Emil Jannings and actress Janet Gaynor.

Aug. 29: The German dirigible *Graf Zeppelin,* carrying 16 passengers and a crew of 37, arrives at Lakehurst, N.J., completing the first round-the-world flight of any kind. It covers 31,400 km in 21 days, seven hours, 26 minutes.

Nov. 18: A 4.5-metre tidal wave strikes Newfoundland's Burin Peninsula, killing 27 people.

Dec. 31: Guy Lombardo and his Royal Canadians open at New York's Roosevelt Hotel, where they will play dance music for decades. A Dec. 31 radio broadcast begins a New Year's Eve tradition.

Guy Lombardo (right) and the Royal Canadians

KAMLOOPS, CIRCA 1920 For more than 50 years, victims of tuberculosis in B.C. got treatment at the Tranquille Sanatorium near Kamloops. Once regarded as among the finest institutions of its kind in North America, the facility closes in 1958 when drug therapies make the combination of rest, sunshine and fresh air unfashionable. This photo shows patients braving winter temperatures to get their fresh-air cure.

Taking the Cure at 33° below Zero

— B.C. Archives B-09834

PEMBERTON, 1925 Sandy and Dell Fowler and kids Billy, Alice, Leonard and Edith, plus Blackie the dog, cross Lillooet River in a dugout canoe. The Fowlers live on the east side of the river and the canoe is one made in Creekside (now Mount Currie) by a native Indian carver. Sandy is public roads foreman and Dell farms the section of land her dad gave her and sells vegetables. The kids also operated a trapline, says *Province* reader Shirley Fowler Brown, who sent us the picture.

VANCOUVER, 1926 The latest in lightweight vacuum cleaners go on sale at Jarvis Electric Co., at Granville and Smithe streets. Signs around the display promote details like a ball-bearing motor that needs no oil, a long-life belt— "no hairpins or loose objects can catch in it" and attachments "for every type of cleaning." "They really clean because of the powerful suction."

— Vancouver Public Library, Special Collections 11526

1920

Western Canada's first air mail is delivered from Seattle to Victoria by float plane.

A traffic count on the Fraser River Bridge shows that about 35 trains cross the bridge daily. On the upper level, 65 automobiles cross every hour.

A fire that started in the residence of the fire chief destroys much of downtown Port Coquitlam.

1921

On March 25, the Capitol Theatre opens on Granville Street.

In September, a crowd of 10,000 watches the dedication of the Peace Arch on the U.S.–Canada border.

Port Coquitlam is damaged in October when a Coquitlam River flood washes away several businesses and St. Catherine's Church.

Richmond is named the cranberry capital of North America.

The census shows B.C.'s population is now 524,582. Males earn an average of $23.87 per week, while females make $14.30.

1922

On New Year's morning, B.C. drivers begin driving on the right-hand side of the street. They previously drove British-style on the left.

Vancouver's first radio broadcast is a news and music program from *Province* Radio-phone.

The Black Candle, an expose of Vancouver's drug trade, is written by Judge Emily Gowan (Ferguson) Murphy. Mrs. Murphy is also known by her pen name, Janey Canuck.

1923

In August, two RCMP agents are charged with illegal possession of opium and opium pipes in Victoria.

In February, 31 men are killed during the night shift at the Canadian Collieries seam of a Cumberland mine.

President Warren Harding visits Vancou-ver—the first time a sitting U.S. president comes to Canada.

While hanging by his heels from the Sun Tower, Harry Houdini escapes from a straightjacket.

— Leonard Frank photo, Jewish Historical Society

— Vancouver Public Library, Special Collections 39487

VANCOUVER, 1927 This cheerful B.C. Telephone Co. lineman is hard at work checking the service from his perch high up a pole in downtown Vancouver. The company is booming, having swallowed up as many as 45 smaller companies to become the only phone service in 1923.

Opposite: **PORT RENFREW, 1926** "Bull Bucker" Archie McHugh leans nonchalantly on a giant spruce which he has just felled for the Cathels and Sorensen Logging Co. in the forests at Port Renfrew on Vancouver Island. McHugh is part of an army of buckers and fallers which is building the logging industry into the backbone of B.C.'s growing economy.

VANCOUVER, 1925 This strangely garbed trio are members of the Imperial Kouncil of Kanadian Knights of Ku Klux Klan. Their getup seems to parody (note the flag displayed) the Klan groups of the southern U.S. However some anti-Semitic, anti–trade union activity did flourish in Saskatchewan in the 1920s, as well as in Vancouver.

1924
Scottish nanny Janet Smith is found murdered at the Osler Street home of prominent businessman F.L. Baker. A Chinese houseboy is accused of the murder, then acquitted.

1925
The Victoria Cougars win the Stanley Cup.

A fur-trimmed ladies' coat costs $18.50, a loaf of bread 10 cents, a 96-piece china dinner set for 12 is $25, and a new Point Grey West bungalow with two bedrooms and hardwood floors is $3,800.

Vancouver puts up its first neon sign.

1926
On Jan. 14, convicted murderers Owen Baker and Harry Sowash are hanged at Oakalla Prison in Burnaby.

West Vancouver's first theatre, the Hollyburn, opens on Marine Drive.

W.C. Shelley builds a road up Grouse Mountain and opens the Grouse Mountain Chalet in September.

1927
B.C.'s first branch library opens in Kitsilano in February.

North Vancouver introduces a 9 p.m. curfew to fight widespread vandalism.

Burnaby volunteer firemen are paid $3 each per fire fought.

1928
Mother Knows Best, Vancouver's first talking picture, opens at the Capitol Theatre on Oct. 20.

Vancouver sprinter Percy Williams wins two gold medals at the Amsterdam Olympics, for the 100 and 200-metre sprints.

1929
In January, 12 senior Vancouver police officers are demoted or dismissed on corruption charges.

On Aug. 7, the first B.C. High School Olympics take place at Hastings Park.

–Melissa Radler

— Vancouver Public Library, Special Collections 6462

VANCOUVER, 1926   The North Shore opens up to Vancouver motorists when the Second Narrows Bridge opens in 1925. Until then the only access was by ferry. By 1926, cars are sharing the bridge with railway trains. They have to give way to trains and to passing ships when the span is lifted.

AMSTERDAM, 1928
On Aug. 1, Vancouver sprinter Percy Williams wins the city's first and second Olympic gold medals in the 100- and 200-metre sprints. He runs the 100 in 10.8 seconds and the 200 in 21.8 seconds and is the first non-American to win both medals. He returns to a hero's welcome and is greeted by thousands in a parade that stretches 2.4 km to Stanley Park.

SURREY, 1927
Travellers to and from the U.S. stop at the customs building at the Pacific Highway border crossing. With its "Welcome to Canada" banner, celebrating the 60th anniversary of confederation, it is a far cry from the truck crossing there today.

— Vancouver Public Library, Special Collections 13295

—City of Surrey Archives 80.12

BOWEN ISLAND, 1922 This happy group of staffers from Spencers Department Store (the pre-cursor to Eaton's) are off on an outing to Bowen Island. Top left is Daisy Wray, who began working in the store's office in 1914. She turned 100 in 1999. The boat trip is on the CPR ship *Princess Patricia*. The picture was sent to us by *Province* reader Valerie McPolin.

VANCOUVER, 1928 Getting your car serviced was just as vital in the 1920s as it is today. This is Blackburn's Service Station and used car lot at the corner of Robson and Seymour streets. Price of that nifty sedan at the front of the lot? $1,195.

— Vancouver City Archives BU P613 N274 #1

Opposite: **1920** Getting a permanent in the 1920s is a hair-raising experience. These early devices are individually wired and it takes a degree of faith and bravery to get perfect curls. But a steely-eyed attendant is on hand in case of emergencies.

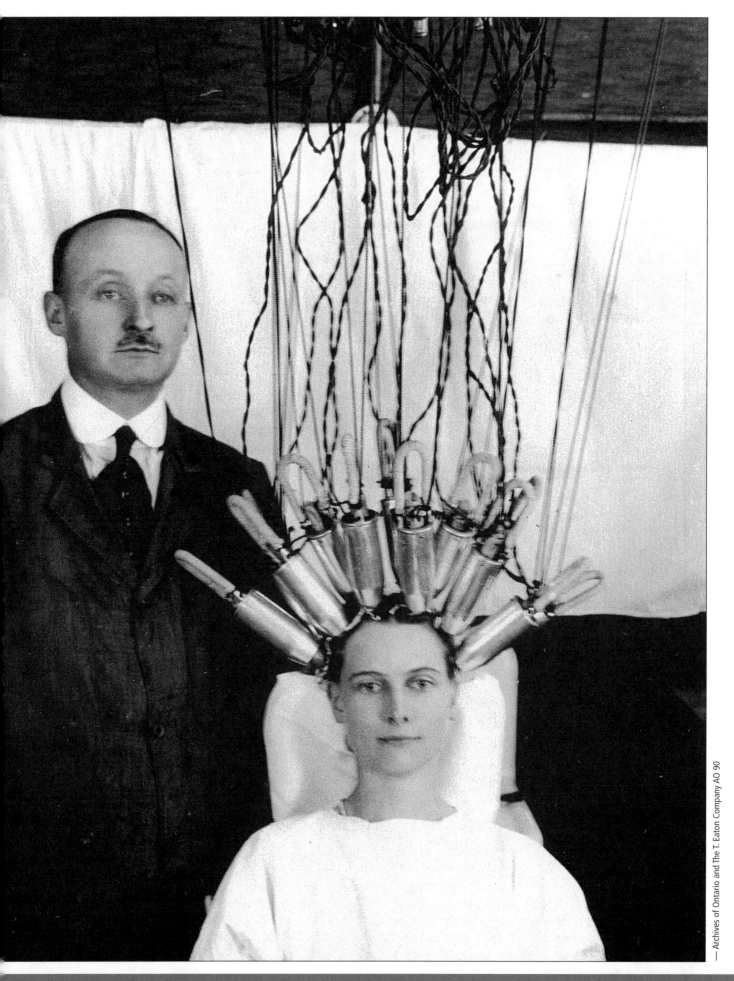

— Archives of Ontario and The T. Eaton Company AO 90

WHITE ROCK, CIRCA 1920 A sunny afternoon attracts a crowd to the pier at White Rock. The completion of the Great Northern's coastal line encourages growing numbers of New Westminster and Vancouver residents to buy summer cottages. Some fathers commute to work in the city aboard a train called the Camper's Special. White Rock pier extends 1,616 feet from shore and has been open since 1914.

— Leonard Frank photo, Jewish Historical Society

— City of Surrey Archives 180.3.15

LULU ISLAND, 1929 These magnificent men and their flying machines sit at the first Vancouver Airport, a year after aviator Charles Lindbergh gives the city and its "less than adequate" fledgling facilities the brush-off. Lindbergh's comments help to spur action to improve the airport. After intensive lobbying, Vancouver voters, keen to get in on the aviation craze, approve a total of $600,000 for airport development, and a new location is selected at the current site on Sea Island.

— Langley Centennial Museum CN950

FORT LANGLEY, 1925 Hundreds of people come to celebrate Fort Langley's centennial on May 2, 1925. They watch a commemorative bronze plaque being placed on a stone cairn to recall the fort's Hudson's Bay Company beginning a century earlier. The Depression had not yet struck and many cars drove to the fort, near the banks of the Fraser River, which had been the only "highway" for most of those 100 years.

An Ogopogo statue in Kelowna bears witness to the numerous reports of sightings.

— Vancouver Public Library, Special Collections 69444

School principal convinced Okanagan demon exists

Sir —

After reading the article in a recent issue of The Province with regard to the "demon" seen in Okanagan Lake, I decided to interview those who had seen the demon with the idea of giving the scoffers who deny that there is such a monster something to consider.

Two of my grandsons with two companions were out on three rafts—some distance from the shore as the surface of the lake that afternoon was still as a pond. That fact affords pretty good proof the boys were not deceived as to what they saw, as they might have been if the surface of the lake had been ruffled by wind.

The boys did not see more than three or four feet of the monster as its head was submerged. They described what they saw as resembling a large stove pipe. When they observed the demon, it was travelling at quite a rate, causing a swell which rocked their rafts.

About this time I was loitering on the wharf when the young lad who was with me called my attention to a swell coming in. The boy remarked that the ferry boat must be starting out from Summerland to Naramata. No boat was in sight and we judged that the swell must have been the same as that which rocked the boys' rafts.

However, I began to think that a big sturgeon might fit the situation. I decided I would interview Mr. James Mitchell, who had seen the serpent a day or two previously. I have known Mr. Mitchell for more than 16 years, and knew I could rely on his description.

Mr. Mitchell stated that he was coming from Penticton to Summerland in his launch when he saw the serpent not more than 200 yards away. He said it was riding in the opposite direction, with its head more than two feet above the surface. Its body was greater in circumference than a large stove pipe, and was dark. The head resembled the head of a snake, and under its jaws its colour was lighter. The head and the three or four feet of its body that was visible was inclined at an angle towards the direction it was travelling. Mr. Mitchell is positive what he saw was not a sturgeon nor any other kind of fish. It had no gills or fins or any of the characteristics of the fish species.

I know there is skepticism regarding our Okanagan sea-serpent, but after interviewing Mr. Mitchell, I am positive that either some form of sea life that has become landlocked, or some prehistoric animal, has been seen repeatedly in the last 30 or 40 years in our Lake Okanagan.

JOHN C. ROBSON
Principal of Rossland Public School
Sept. 6, 1925

Protection for the people

Sir—

In a city of 400,000 people not far away, the hold-up men became a public menace. The city police magistrate determined that citizens and visitors should be protected from robbery and ill usage. He publicly announced that all future hold-up men, in addition to a jail sentence, would receive 25 lashes with the cat-o'-nine tails.

Several days passed and five of this class were caught, thanks to a proficient police force, and they received the medicine aforesaid, which was also announced in the press.

Suffice it to say, that city's atmosphere cleared quickly and peace reigned supreme. The big fellow at the jail who administered the cat said he really enjoyed the job and would keep in training.

A READER
Sept. 6, 1925

Insolence at U.S. border

Sir—

I note a letter in a recent issue of the Sunday Province. I would like to most heartily corroborate all this lady says regarding U.S. immigration officials. I have travelled extensively about the world, and in no country, save the U.S. have I met with anything but courtesy and civility from immigration or customs officials.

But at almost every port of entry to the U.S. one finds the same thing—a collection of insolent, vulgar "jerks-in-office" from whom one is forced to submit to a coarse, ill-bred insolence unparalleled in those of any other nationality on earth. We may indeed be truly thankful we live under the Union Jack, which stands for real freedom, decency and civilized manners.

S.O. BEESON
Qualicum Beach, Aug. 2, 1925

Reform the youth

Sir —

The seven-year sentence passed upon Fred Campbell, the 18-year-old boy who tried to rob a bank at gunpoint, makes one wonder whether the purpose of Canadian "justice" is revenge or crime prevention.

He said they wouldn't get him so easily next time. They won't. Seven years in the penitentiary will turn this adventurous, wayward boy into a wary criminal with a resolution to avenge those years upon society at large. Seven years in the penitentiary will not teach him honesty and a sense of fair play.

He is plucky and took his sentence calmly. We are giving him time to think it over and realize its monstrous unfairness.

Why couldn't the Canadian Bank of Commerce refuse to prosecute, give him a position of trust on a decent salary, put him on his honour and make a man of him?

I am not a sentimental woman. I said and still believe that the Leopold Loeb boys should have been shot as one shoots mad dogs.

Hanging would not be much worse to a boy of his type than seven years' confinement.

STELLA MEADE
Sept. 6, 1925

(Richard Loeb and Nathan Leopold were two Chicago 18-year-olds convicted in 1924 of murdering a 13-year-old boy for kicks. They escaped the gallows only because their attorney, Clarence Darrow, successfully argued that homosexuality was grounds for insanity—Editor)

Clean up or quit

Sir—

You are to be commended for your editorial regarding the raids pulled off on bootleggers by the provincial police a few days ago. Attorney-General Manson did the right thing in showing up the city police. The city police are fully aware of the location of these dives, and if they can not clean them up and keep them clean, they should be replaced by those who can. It's time the people of this city awoke to the fact that they are paying the police to do their duty, and insist that they give the service required or get out.

H. EDWARDS
Vancouver, Jan. 18, 1925

Too many holdups

Sir—

About a week ago there were published some remarks by Mayor Taylor to the effect that he hoped to arrange matters so that the police would spend more time on the streets in an endeavour to reduce the number of burglaries and holdups, instead of raiding Chinese gambling dens. The mayor's proposal met with the unqualified approval of many citizens.

Since then, there have appeared accounts of a number of cases of women being molested or held up on the streets, and accounts of raids by the police on gambling dens, in one of which 74 Chinese were rounded up.

Apart from the fact that other residents of Vancouver, so long as they are not Chinese, can gamble to their hearts' content, at mah jong, bridge, or any other game, without the police interfering with them, it is outrageous that women should be attacked so frequently on our streets as they have been this winter.

I do hope the citizens of Vancouver will support Mayor Taylor in his efforts to have the streets better patrolled by police.

E.O.
March 1, 1925

Boys adopt hopscotch

Sir—

This is a decadent age, but I was more than astonished to find that the games of the modern boy are becoming effeminate.

The good, old-fashioned game of "nobbies," I am informed by a lad of 14, is now unknown, and instead of such manly, vigorous exercise, the lads of the day are playing—what do you think?—hopscotch!

Why, sir, when I was a youth even girls hesitated to play hopscotch. I am informed, however, that games that were formerly considered masculine such as baseball, soccer and lacrosse are now essayed by girls.

Perhaps this is the reason why girls are becoming more sturdy and assertive, while boys are taking to floppy trousers and frilled shirts.

ALISTAIR MacALLISTER
Sept. 6, 1925

— Vancouver Public Library, Special Collections 1294

Vancouver, 1938

Vancouver police ride the running boards of a squad car (rushing through the wash of a street-cleaning truck) on their way to the post office. When police arrive they find that the occupation of the post office has turned into a bloody riot. The occupants are protesting the province's discontinuation of relief for the unemployed and dismal conditions in relief camps run by the Department of National Defence.

UNREST AMONG THE UNEMPLOYED

BY DAMIAN INWOOD

As the Dirty Thirties get under way, B.C. is Canada's wealthiest province with a per capita income of $4,339.

As the Depression deepens, the Unemployment Relief Act is passed by the House of Commons on Sept. 22, 1930.

Federal government relief camps for transient unemployed men are home to 20,000 men nationwide. The camps are run by the Dept. of National Defence and enforce military-style discipline. Camp dwellers receive 20 cents per day.

The latest celestial discovery is that of the planet Pluto by U.S. astronomer Clyde Tombaugh.

The Vancouver Art Gallery is founded in 1931, and Canada's population tops 10 million, with B.C. at 694,000.

The Co-operative Commonwealth Federation, the forerunner to the New Democratic Party, is formed in Calgary by socialist and independent MPs in 1932.

In May 1934, a miracle puts Callander, Ont., on the world map.

Elzire Dionne gives birth to five babies, known as the Dionne Quintuplets. They are the first surviving quintuplets in history, and Dr. Allan

Roy Dafoe becomes an international celebrity.

In ensuing years, the quintuplets' parents, Elzire and Oliva Dionne, are pushed into the background as the province takes over the children's care, putting them on display to thousands of visitors clamouring to see the babies.

Canadian Dr. Norman Bethune goes to Spain in 1936 to serve as a medical officer for the Republican forces in the Spanish Civil War. He revolutionizes battlefield medicine by developing the first mobile blood transfusion service.

In Quebec the following year, the "Padlock Law" comes into force. It allows authorities to padlock any building if it is suspected of being used to "propagate communism."

As the decade continues, a dark shadow spreads over Europe as Adolf Hitler and his Nazi thugs launch their attacks on Jews in Germany.

Canadian Prime Minister Mackenzie King pays a visit to Hitler and describes him as being "a simple sort of peasant" who poses no serious threat.

Two years later, after Hitler invades Poland, Canada declares war on Germany on Sept. 10, 1939.

> After Hitler invades Poland, Canada declares war on Germany on Sept. 10, 1939

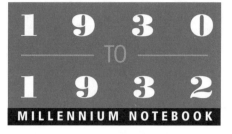

1930

Jan. 5: Josef Stalin starts collective agriculture in the Soviet Union. All land, livestock and equipment now belong to the state. A family can own a house, garden, stable and one cow.

Feb. 18: A 24-year-old amateur astronomer, Clyde William Tombaugh, discovers the planet Pluto.

Feb. 20: Cairine Wilson, a Women's Liberal Club organizer, is appointed Canada's first woman senator. In 1949 she is appointed Canada's first woman delegate to the UN.

April 6: Mohandas K. Gandhi arrives at Dandi, on the western coast of India, completing a "march to the sea" to harvest salt illegally from the ocean.

May 16: Gilbert LaBine, a prospector at Great Bear Lake in the Northwest Territories, discovers pitchblende which is a source of uranium and radium.

July: Uruguay hosts and wins the first World Cup of soccer.

Aug. 16: The first British Empire Games, later renamed the Commonwealth Games, begin in Hamilton, Ont.

1931

Jan. 8: Pope Pius XI issues an encyclical denouncing trial marriages, all forms of birth control and divorce.

May 1: The Empire State Building opens in New York. At 102 storeys it will be the tallest building in the world for 40 years.

Sept. 8: Coal miners go on strike in Estevan, Sask. On Sept. 29, three stikers are killed in clashes with the RCMP.

Oct. 24: Chicago gang lord Al Capone is sentenced to 11 years in prison—for tax evasion.

Nov. 12: Maple Leaf Gardens opens in Toronto.

Dec. 11: The Statute of Westminster is passed by the British Parliament giving Canada full control over its domestic laws and external affairs. The Governor

Buddy, can you spare a dime?

Few countries are hit as hard by the Great Depression as Canada.

As businesses fail, one in five Canadians goes on government relief during the Dirty Thirties and 30 per cent are unemployed.

Between 1929 and 1933, Canada's gross national expenditure drops by 42 per cent.

Because of the drop in world markets for exports, the four western provinces are battered hardest.

Saskatchewan is plagued by crop failures and the lowest price for wheat in recorded history.

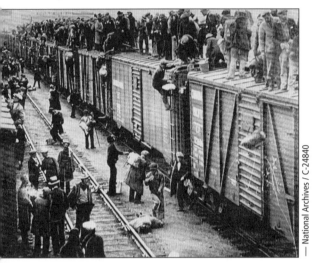

— National Archives / C-24840

June 1935: En route to Ottawa, some 1,800 jobless men stop at Regina.

Provincial income plunges by 90 per cent in two years, forcing two-thirds of the rural population to seek government help.

Canada's birth rate drops from 13.1 live births per thousand in 1930 to 9.7 in 1937.

Monthly relief rates for a family of five vary from $60 in Calgary to $19 in Halifax.

Diseases such as scurvy are common.

Hobos ride the rails, looking for handouts and greener pastures, and the government sets up unemployment relief camps for single, homeless men who can't get help from local governments.

General becomes the Crown's representative in Canada.

1932

May 2: *The Jack Benny Show,* featuring the violinist-comedian, premieres on NBC.

May 21: Amelia Earhart lands in Northern Ireland, becoming the first woman to fly solo across the Atlantic.

May 26: The Canadian Radio Broadcasting Commission, forerunner to the Canadian Broadcasting Corporation, is established by Parliament. In 1933 the CRBC begins transmitting in English and French from Montreal.

July 7: The Dow Jones Industrial Average dips to an all-time low of 41.22.

Aug. 1: The Co-operative Commonwealth Federation, or CCF, is founded in Calgary as the first major democrat-

ic socialist party in Canada, led by James Shaver Woods-worth. It is the forerunner of the New Democratic Party.

Nov. 8: Americans, desperate for change, elect New York Gov. Franklin Delano Roosevelt president.

Amelia Earhart

PASSAGES

THOMAS ALVA EDISON

Inventions that sprang from his fertile brain had a profound effect on the 20th century. Whenever we turn on a light, watch a film or listen to a record, we can thank a home-schooled, voracious reader named Thomas Edison. Working out of a laboratory in Menlo Park, N.J., in 1876, and later in an "invention factory" in West Orange, N.J., Edison and his staff toiled over as many as 40 projects at a time and applied for nearly 400 patents a year. He invented the light bulb, phonograph, movie projector, celluloid film, talking movies and carbon microphones. He was issued patents for 1,093 inventions—more than any other person in U.S. history.

TRANSPORTATION

THE 'PEOPLE'S CAR'

The Volkswagen, or "people's car," is introduced in Germany. Built from a design by Ferdinand Porsche, the simple, inexpensive automobile is Adolf Hitler's answer to Henry Ford's Model T. Germany will begin mass-producing the bubble-shaped, rear-engine vehicle in 1937.

ENTERTAINMENT

THE FIRST DRIVE-IN MOVIE

Noting society's fascination with movies and cars, Richard Hollingshead Jr. combines the two and in 1933 patents his drive-in movie theatre. He experiments in the driveway at his house in Camden, N.J., mounting a 1928 Kodak projector on the hood of his car and projecting films onto a screen nailed to trees. America's first drive-in theatre opens in Camden in June. The first drive-in in Canada opens in Hamilton in 1946.

ENTERTAINMENT

THE CINEMA'S BEST YEAR

In 1939, Canadian movie fans experience one of the greatest of all years for films. *The Wizard of Oz,* MGM's version of a children's classic, starring Judy Garland, and *Gone with the Wind,* with Vivien Leigh as Scarlett O'Hara and Clark Gable as Rhett Butler (above), are huge hits. When *Gone with the Wind* premieres in Atlanta Dec. 15, 1939, several women faint when Gable appears.

GREY OWL'S SECRET

The film boom of the 1930s included several productions featuring a Canadian Indian named Grey Owl, who turns out to be an Englishman named Archie Belaney.

He became a celebrated environmentalist of the 1930s and his original identity was not revealed until after he died.

HEROES IN TIGHTS

The man of steel from the planet Krypton makes his comic-book debut in the June 1938 issue of Action Comics. Superman is the brainchild of two 24-year-old cartoonists. They are Toronto Star artist Joe Shuster and American Jerry Siegel. "Mild-mannered reporter" Clark Kent transforms himself into Superman by ducking into a phone booth and then bounding about in blue tights and a red cape fighting for "truth, justice and the American way."

LEGENDS

THE MAD TRAPPER

The RCMP take part in a 48-day running battle with Albert Johnson, over 240 kilometres along the Arctic Circle, before finally killing The Mad Trapper of Rat River. RCMP are called to Johnson's cabin when there are complaints he's been tampering with traplines.

A shootout ensues and by the time the Mounties get their man, with the help of an airplane on Feb. 17, 1932, he has killed one man and seriously wounded two more in four shootouts.

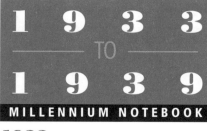

1933 TO 1939
MILLENNIUM NOTEBOOK

1933

May 27: Dubbed the "Century of Progress," the 1933 Chicago World's Fair attracts 22 million visitors during its run from May 27 to Nov. 12. Much of the fair's success is credited to fan dancer Sally Rand, who appears in the "Streets of Paris" attraction. Carrying feathery plumes or a giant opaque balloon, an apparently naked Rand sashays across the stage to Claude Debussy's "Clair de Lune," titillating the audience without ever showing more than her face, arms and legs.

July 14: The National Socialists are declared the only legal political party in Germany. It announces a program to perfect the "Aryan race" by sterilizing people deemed unworthy of breeding. Thousands of Jews are sent to concentration camps for "consorting with German girls."

Dec. 2: Newfoundland loses its status as a Dominion, due to financial problems, and reverts to being a Crown colony.

1934

Oct. 16: Mao Tse-tung, leader of the Chinese Communists, begins what will be called "The Long March," an epic year-long trek of 9,600 kilometres across 18 mountain ranges and six major rivers. Mao leads his 90,000-strong army north to Yenan province. About 68,000 Communist soldiers die along the way.

1935

March 11: The Bank of Canada begins operations.

June 5: About 1,000 unemployed men from government work camps board freight cars in Vancouver to begin the "On to Ottawa Trek." The trek ends in a riot in Regina on July 1.

Sept. 3: British speed ace Sir Malcolm Campbell sets a world land-speed record of 301.337 m.p.h. in *Bluebird* at Bonneville Flats, Utah.

Sept. 15: Adolf Hitler signs the Nuremberg Laws rescinding civil rights for Germany's 600,000 Jews, the first stage of his "final solution" to rid Europe of all Jews.

1936

July 18: Civil war erupts in Spain as army commanders in Morocco begin a revolt against the weak government in Madrid. Within Spain, Francisco Franco takes command of the Falangists (Spanish fascists) in armed opposition to the Loyalists. The Spanish Civil War becomes a glorious cause for many young idealists who travel to Spain to fight.

Sept. 14: Ontario nurse Dorothea Parker is arrested for distributing birth-control information.

Nov. 2: The Canadian Broadcasting Corporation is created to replace the Canadian Radio Broadcasting Commission.

Dec. 11: The 325-day reign of England's Edward VIII ends when he renounces the throne in favour of "the woman I love," American divorcee Wallis Simpson. Edward's brother, the Duke of York, becomes George VI.

1937

April 26: "King of Swing" Benny Goodman has teenagers screaming at the Paramount Theatre, New York.

German bombers, helping fascists in the Spanish Civil War, devastate the town of Guernica, near Bilbao, killing hundreds of civilians. Pablo Picasso is inspired to paint *Guernica,* depicting the horrors of war.

May 6: The German dirigible *Hindenburg,* considered the crowning achievement of the Third Reich, bursts into flames at the naval air station in Lakehurst, N.J. Of 97 passengers and crew, 36 die and most are injured. Radio reporter Herbert Morrison's eyewitness account, with the plaintive cry, "Oh, the humanity," is the first recorded news report broadcast nationally by NBC radio.

May 27: San Francisco's Golden Gate Bridge, proclaimed as the "eighth wonder of the world," is officially opened.

June 29: Joseph-Armand Bombardier patents the snowmobile, a seven-passenger machine costing $7,500.

July 1: About 1,300 Canadian volunteers join the Mackenzie-Papineau Battalion to support the Spanish government against General Franco. Dr. Norman Bethune, one of the Canadian volunteers, leads a blood-transfusion service during the Civil War. In April 1937, the Canadian government

---

Canada at war again

When Hitler invades Poland, it is finally clear his word cannot be trusted. Canada declares war on Germany on Sept. 10, 1939, seven days after Britain and France.

At this time, Canada's military comprises only 4,500 regulars and 60,000 militia reserves, plus 4,500 in the RCAF and a Royal Canadian Navy of 1,800 and 13 ships.

In September, the first Canadian troops leave for Europe after Ottawa decides to send one Canadian division to Britain.

Many more will follow.

By November a Canadian Military HQ is set up in London.

In December, the British Commonwealth Air Training Plan is established to train aircrews from Canada, Britain, Australia and New Zealand. By the end of the war 130,000 airmen have been trained at bases in Canada.

Right: Waving a peace agreement with Hitler that soon proves to be worthless, British Prime Minister Neville Chamberlain makes his famous 'peace in our time' speech on returning to England in 1938.

— Associated Press

German pride takes a heavy blow when the airship Hindenburg bursts into flames in New Jersey in 1937 during a live radio broadcast.

creates a law forbidding Canadian participation in foreign wars.

Aug. 8: As war between China and Japan heats up, Peking falls to the Japanese invaders and army rule is established.

Sept. 1: Trans-Canada Air Lines, later to become Air Canada, begins regular flights between Vancouver and Seattle.

Nov. 24: The Gorvernor General's Literary Awards are established by the Canadian Authors' Association.

Dec. 25: Walt Disney's *Snow White and the Seven Dwarfs*, the first full-length animated cartoon, opens.

1938

Feb. 24: A toothbrush developed by DuPont Co. becomes the first nylon-based product.

July 15: A Manhattan ticker-tape parade welcomes Howard Hughes a day after the Houston-born millionaire and his four-man crew establish a record for around-the-world flight—three days, 19 hours, eight minutes.

Sept. 2: Adolf Hitler scores a victory, following a week-long conference in Munich, when he and Italian dictator Benito Mussolini gain concessions from British Prime Minister Neville Chamberlain and French Premier Edouard Daladier. The agreement returns Sudetenland to Germany from Czechoslovakia and Chamberlain goes home to assure England of "peace in our time."

Nov. 9: Young Nazis rampage in Berlin, smashing windows of Jewish stores in Kristallnacht, or Crystal Night. A pogrom follows in which more than 90 Jews are killed and between 20,000 and 30,000 more are sent to concentration camps.

1939

Jan. 26: Gen. Franco's rebel army occupies Barcelona, ending the three-year Spanish Civil War. Franco's camp is recognized as the official government of Spain.

VANCOUVER GENERAL HOSPITAL, 1939 In late May, King George VI and Queen Elizabeth make a royal visit to Vancouver and open both the Lions Gate Bridge and the third and present Hotel Vancouver (where they stay for one night in royal style). Here, patients from Vancouver General Hospital seem to enjoy the royal couple's curbside manner, clapping and waving Union Jacks from the discomfort of their sick beds.

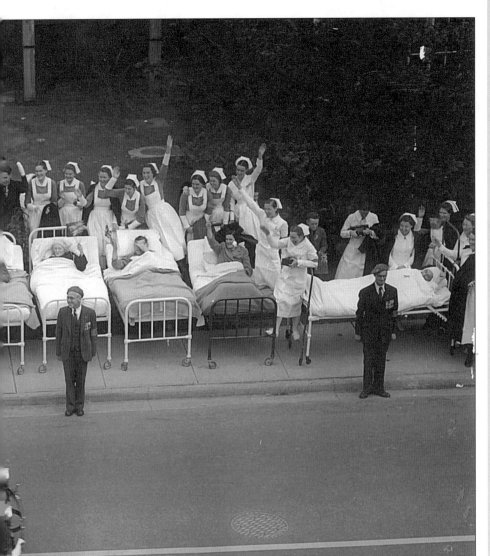

— Vancouver Public Library, Special Collections 24941

1930

The freighter *Pacific Gatherer* crashes into the Second Narrows Bridge on Sept. 19, causing $250,000 damage and closing the bridge to all traffic until June 1934.

An explosion at Blakeburn mine in Princeton kills 45.

No Drone, a hen from Whiting farm in Surrey, sets the world record in egg-laying by producing 357 eggs in 365 days.

On Nov. 1, Victoria switches to dial telephones. Vancouver follows suit nine years later.

1931

Kitsilano's salt-water swimming pool, the largest in North America, opens Aug. 15.

West Vancouver sells 1,600 hectares of land to a syndicate, British Properties, at $47 per hectare.

1932

On Feb. 22, 6,000 men, women and children, many flying red Soviet Union flags, stage a "hunger march" from Powell Street to Cambie Street. Having been hit hard by the Depression, the marchers demand $25 per week in unemployment insurance.

Starting June 1, driver's licences cost $1 each.

B.C. high jumper Duncan McNaughton wins a gold medal at the Los Angeles Olympics.

The Burrard Street Bridge opens July 1.

1933

Newspapers sell for three cents a copy.

Jimmy McLarnin, from Union Street in Vancouver, becomes the world welterweight boxing champion.

On June 9, a bylaw amendment allows men to go shirtless and wear bathing trunks on Vancouver beaches.

Nat Bailey founds White Spot No. 1 restaurant at 67th and Granville.

1934

Food relief rates are raised to $30 per month for a family of five.

— Leonard Frank photo, Jewish Historical Society

1935

Vancouver Mayor G.G. McGeer decrees Jan. 6 a day of prayer for forgiveness of city sins.

On Jan. 20, Vancouver gets 17.5 inches of snow in 24 hours. The roof of Hastings Park Forum collapses.

An April 23, a relief camp parade protesting low wages results in $5,000 damage at the Hudson's Bay Company on Granville.

The Kitsilano Showboat opens.

Sunkist oranges are 69 cents for three dozen, British Consol's roll-your-own cigarette tobacco is 90 cents per half-pound tin, and a Ford V8 truck is $760.

B.C. is spending more than $8 million annually on relief.

Protesting relief camp conditions, 1,000 unemployed men board freight trains on June 3 to begin the "On to Ottawa" trek.

1936

Two thousand women sign a petition for free government-run birth-control clinics.

Vancouver is linked to London, England, by telegraph wires.

Gasoline is 25 cents per gallon.

1937

The Oak movie theatre opens at Kingsway and Marlborough. Tickets cost 25 cents for adults, 10 cents for kids.

1938

Vancouver police order a crackdown on Chinese gambling dens.

Ann Mundigel is the first person to swim from Vancouver to Bowen Island.

1939

King George VI and Queen Elizabeth pay a royal visit to Vancouver and 600,000 people line the May 29 procession route.

The month-long return tour across Canada starts in Quebec and ends in Halifax.

–Hardip Johal

VANCOUVER, 1938 Bustle, bustle outside the bus terminal. Pacific Stage Lines' new Clipper Stage Coach rounds the corner on to Seymour Street (above). The corner of Dunsmuir and Seymour was as busy in '38 as it is today. Note the 'exotic' destination designations affixed to the building (the upper floor of which is now the popular Railway Club bar).

Opposite: **STEVESTON, CIRCA 1935** Percy Bicknell poses with mallards and pintails shot on a duck-hunting expedition to the local marshes. Bicknell, born in 1897, worked for B.C. Packers for 43 years but his passion was hunting. He supplied ducks and geese to local butchers and was a well-known carver of decoys and a builder of Fraser River duck punts. Bicknell died in 1959. His son, *Province* reader R.H. Bicknell, provided this photograph from the family album.

VANCOUVER POST OFFICE, 1938 On June 19, 'Bloody Sunday,' Vancouver police use clubs and tear gas to evict unemployed men from the post office at Granville and Hastings, ending a six-week protest against relief stoppage to the unemployed.

— Vancouver Public Library, Special Collections 1313

— The Province

— The Province

LONSDALE QUAY, 1938 Cars and foot passengers line up for the next ferry from Lonsdale Quay.

Opposite: **LIONS GATE BRIDGE, 1938** Construction is well under way on the span between Vancouver and North Vancouver, as this July 13 photograph, looking north from the south end of the bridge, illustrates. Three hundred men are employed to finish the project. The Lions Gate Bridge, the longest suspension bridge in the British Empire at the time, will be completed four months later and open to traffic on Nov. 12. The bridge, which costs more than $5 million to build and carries a 25-cent automobile toll, is officially opened May 26, 1939.

— Leonard Frank photo, Jewish Historical Society

FALSE CREEK FLATS, 1931 The Reverend Andrew Roddan (left) of First United Church visits Chinese squatters at a makeshift cookhouse in the False Creek flats. The squalid area is called the 'jungle' during the Depression, and the shanties it contains are the only homes homeless men can find.

7905-1
MOORE
Co.

— Vancouver City Archives RE P13 N7

QUESNEL GOLF CLUB, 1939
Lloyd Harper (wearing tie) and Jack Smedley buddy up for a round on the links during the Cariboo Open Golf Tournament in the fall of '39. "This picture epitomizes what golf is all about —two buddies playing for the love of the game," writes *Province* reader Glenys Pumfrey, whose father was Lloyd Harper. "Our green fees have definitely gone up!" Indeed they have — note the 50-cents-a-day green fees.

— City of Surrey Archives 180.9.08

PACIFIC HIGHWAY, CLOVERDALE, 1935
A lone car plows its way through the flood waters after a severe ice and snow storm strikes the Fraser Valley in January, causing extensive flooding. The deluge cuts communication and transportation links throughout the region.

SPANISH BANKS, 1933 Resembling a hearse rally more than a day at the beach, this shot of Spanish Banks shows how 1930s families spent weekend afternoons. This is the year that Vancouver city council allowed men to go topless on city beaches. You can see children enjoying tidal pools, and Vancouver's emerging skyline in the background.

VANCOUVER, 1939 All is calm in this wintertime panorama looking northwest across the city. Fishing boats traverse the harbour, fresh snow tops the mountains and the trees surrender their leaves to the cold. But in September of '39, Vancouver Harbour is put under control of the Royal Canadian Navy. Gun emplacements are built under the Lions Gate Bridge and at strategic points along the west coast of B.C. All shipping passing into the harbour must stop and report to naval launches.

—Vancouver Public Library, Special Collections 6175

—Vancouver Public Library, Special Collections 6189

No more noise

Sir—

Now that we have a new fire-eating mayor, perhaps he will have the bells at the Twelfth Avenue and Granville Street intersection stopped when people want to sleep.

Only a few cities in America still use bells on their traffic signals.

J.W.N.
Jan. 5, 1935

How quick is a flash?

Sir—

It is incredible that a man of the education and prominence of Mr. Herridge, Canadian ambassador at Washington, could express himself as reported in addressing a convention at Montreal recently.

He is quoted as saying: "Had I the power, I would throw over our economic system in a flash, if I thought there was a better one available," which is like a tramp saying to his mate while trying to be cheerful over a slim breakfast: "Say, Bill, if we had some ham we'd have ham and eggs, if we had some eggs." Mr. Herridge knows he has not "the power" and that he does not think there is any better system in sight. Moreover, throwing "over our economic system in a flash" recalls the description of Noah Webster as "a famous man who, in a moment of inspiration, dashed off a dictionary."

Surely our public men and the press have a responsibility in uttering and publishing such things.

SIMPLE SIMON
Jan. 5, 1935

Stool-pigeon or good citizen?

Sir—

Why do we have so many criminals in Vancouver? Is it because the public does not care? If we want a clean city, let us do our duty and help the police crush

— Vancouver Public Library, Special Collections 6636

When the letter below was written, Vancouver Mayor Gerry McGeer, above, had just roared into office with the biggest majority in city history and was soon well known for his bombast and autocratic approach.

Kill the poll tax

Sir—

Now that we have a man of action in Mayor McGeer, I trust he will put his foot down on one of the most miserable taxes, the poll tax, especially in the case of returned men, who saw action on any of the several fronts, and did their part during the crisis of 1914-1918.

Lord only knows there are hundreds of returned men in the city who have troubles enough without this miserable tax being added to their worries.

ONE OF THEM
Jan. 19, 1935

criminals. Make Vancouver hell for the criminal and a paradise for the law-abiding citizen. But any person not wearing the uniform or badge of law and order, willing to help the police, is called a stool-pigeon, a rat and a squealer, etc. Why? Can anyone tell me why?

If I see a person commit a crime or know the hideout of criminals sought by police,

should I keep mum and try to convince myself that it is not my business? What would you do—help the offender and be a good citizen, or help the law and be called a rat? I will help the law.

GEO. HOLMBERGH
Jan. 5, 1935

Vancouver's Hitler

Sir—

I would suggest that the lawyers go further than the B.C. Legislature in their present inquiry and try to have passed a law barring mayors of any city in the Dominion from a seat in the legislature or federal Parliament. Had such a law been in effect, recent degrading events in this city would not have happened. A dangerous precedent has been created and, if ignored, will be followed throughout the country. That a mere mayor should intimidate the government of the province and encroach on matters in the church's province is almost unbelievable. Truly fools step in, etc.

History repeats itself. A man called Hitler once asked for power and still more power, so that he might alleviate the conditions of his countrymen. And what use has he made of it? Exactly what might have been expected. He destroyed all liberty, freedom, decency, and raised all his own friends and adherents to affluent positions. Our mayor is doubtless well read in these tactics.

G. HAMILTON
1583 Barclay street
Jan. 19, 1935

Pipe 'em down

Sir—

As the Vancouver police force appears to experience considerable difficulty in dealing with crime in the orthodox manner, and as I understand there are a hundred or more Scotsmen in the Vancouver police force, why not let these men patrol their beats on the streets with their bagpipes?

One hundred pipers and a' and a'
Might frighten the bandits awa', awa'!

A.O.G.
Jan. 5, 1935

Here's a chance!

Sir—

Since this seems to be the era of reforms, let me put forth my plan to feed, clothe and warm our unemployed. My project would need the generous assistance of the B.C. Electric and the B.C. Telephone companies. All I would want them to do is to take down all the telephone poles and bury the power and telephone wires. The poles that would be discarded could be cut up and sent to needy families for firewood. Of course, there would be many men employed in this project, so nearly all the unemployed in the city would be put to work. I think we should start right away.

Gerry and I should get together.

D.A.C.M.
Jan. 19, 1935

The joy of serving

Sir—

One morning recently my boy and I decided it would be nice to give a bicycle which he had outgrown to another boy whose father was not in any too comfortable circumstances. We had painted the bike bright red and found it needed a few mechanical adjustments. So I went to our local repairman with the bike.

The repairman swept me off my feet with his exuberance. Didn't I think this was the most glorious morning ever? He was so delighted with the sunshine he said he could have danced on the housetops. In the meantime he is busy repairing and adjusting the bike. He says: "You see, I am responsible to all the kids in this district for their bikes. They bring them to me when they have trouble and I fix them. They pay me if they can and if they can't, well it is all right too. They are all my friends. My, how lonesome I would be without them!"

In walked a boy with a bike with a carrier on it, almost in tears. He had expected to make some money that day delivering parcels, but his bike had failed him and would take several hours to repair. The repairman gave him a glance and assured him there was nothing to worry about. Within a minute he was out with another bike with a carrier, loaned to him so he could carry on.

My bike was ready by this time and I was asked if 15 cents was too much. I fully expected to pay at least 50 cents. I asked him how business had been, and that was one of the reasons for his jubilance. He said: "You see, I have sold 17 bikes for Christmas and they have to be delivered tonight. I have an old touring car to make these deliveries."

If it had rained he would only have been able to pack in two or three bikes at a time, but it was such a glorious day he would be able to put his top down and load up the back. "Can you imagine the fun I am going to have tonight rolling along in my old touring car with the top down delivering these bikes?"

Santa Claus himself could not have looked forward to the event with more pleasure.

Most of us would not envy the life of a bicycle repairman. I envy this man the happiness and joy he gets out of life in the spirit of service.

I am going to visit this man more often. There is a lot I can learn from him about the joy of giving.

WEST POINT
Jan. 5, 1935

—Vancouver Public Library, Special Collections 44965

North Vancouver, 1942

The threat of war is brought home to schoolchildren when they are issued gas masks and take part in evacuation drills. These students at St. Mary's School in North Vancouver are rehearsing for a possible attack after the Japanese bombing of Pearl Harbor raised fears that B.C. might be a target.

THE WAR HITS HOME

By Damian Inwood

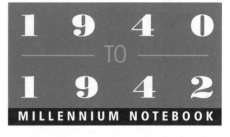

anada is at war in Europe, but back home in B.C. the demand for ships and aircraft sparks a boom.

Factories spring up around Vancouver, employing more than 30,000 in shipbuilding alone.

With men away at war, women move into the workplace and by 1943, 1,500 women work in shipyards, 1,100 in three Boeing plants and more than 1,000 in mills around the city.

Johnny Canuck makes his debut as a comic-book war hero.

After the Dec. 7, 1941, Japanese attack on Pearl Harbour, fear and suspicion mount against Japanese-Canadians on the West Coast.

Three months later, 22,000 Japanese are ordered removed from their homes and relocated to camps in the Interior.

Their homes, 1,350 fishing boats, businesses and personal possessions are seized and auctioned off to unscrupulous entrepreneurs.

The anti-Japanese sentiment is further fuelled by an incident in which a Japanese submarine is alleged to have fired several shells at Estevan Point lighthouse on Vancouver Island.

The story is used to justify Prime Minister Mackenzie King's decision to intern Japanese-Canadians for posing a threat to Canada.

Meanwhile, Vancouver develops a kind of siege mentality as wartime measures come into vogue and 10,000 volunteers show up to join Air Raid Protection groups.

A blackout is initiated, while gasoline and butter rationing are introduced.

People celebrate Meatless Wednesdays, while women use leg makeup instead of nylons and men's pant-cuffs are banned to conserve fabric.

When the Second World War ends, the heroes come home and the baby boom starts.

Due to a lack of housing, a home-building boom also begins.

As the decade nears its end, Canada starts cutting its ties with Mother England.

In 1949 the Supreme Court becomes the court of last resort for all cases heard in Canada. Up until that year, the Judicial Committee of the Privy Council in Britain could still hear civil cases.

Newfoundland enters the Dominion of Canada as its 10th province.

> After the Dec. 7, 1941, Japanese attack on Pearl Harbour, fear and suspicion mount against Japanese-Canadians on the West Coast

1940

Jan. 4: In Dublin, Irish Premier Eamon de Valera is granted full powers to counter terrorism by the Irish Republican Army.

May 13: In his "blood, toil, tears and sweat" speech to the Commons, Prime Minister Winston Churchill declares Britain's aim against Germany: "Victory at all costs, victory in spite of all terror, victory however long and hard the road may be: For without victory, there is no survival."

May 26: The Allies undertake a desperate evacuation from the beaches of France at Dunkirk. Over 10 days, an armada of small boats plucks 340,000 Allied soldiers off the beaches.

June 14: The Nazis occupy Paris. The next day, the Nazi flag is raised over Versailles and Hitler is there, dancing a jig at the success of the Third Reich's power.

July 11: Unemployment insurance is introduced in Canada to help workers who lose their jobs through no fault of their own. It goes into effect on July 1, 1941.

Aug. 23: Canadian citizens of German and Italian origin who arrived in Canada after Sept. 1, 1922, lose their naturalized status and must report to the police as enemy aliens.

Sept. 1: The first group of German prisoners of war arrive in Canada from Britain, to be interned in Canadian POW camps.

Sept. 15: The BBC reports 185 German planes downed in a single day. For two months the skies over London, Manchester and Liverpool have presented a deadly aerial circus, with British fighters taking on—and knocking out—Germany's Stuka bombers.

1941

March 28: British writer Virginia Woolf drowns herself near her home in Sussex, England. She is clinically depressed and unable to face another nervous breakdown and institutionalization.

May 27: After a high-seas chase of 2,816 kilometres, a Royal Navy flotilla corners

and sinks the battleship *Bismarck*, pride of the German navy.

June 22: Germany launches Operation Barbarossa, an invasion of the Soviet Union along a 2,900-kilometre front.

July 1: Modern commercial television is born when NBC and CBS begin transmitting 15 hours per week of cartoons, sports and news from New York City.

Dec. 7: Japanese airplanes attack the Pacific fleet of the U.S. navy at Pearl Harbour, Hawaii, in a surprise raid. Losses are high: 2,330 servicemen and 100 civilians, four battleships and 11 other ships sunk or critically disabled and 188 aircraft destroyed on the ground.

Four days later, the U.S. Congress declares war on Japan.

Winston Churchill and his famous 'V for victory' sign

Dec. 25: Hong Kong falls to Japan. More than 500 captured Canadians will later die in Japanese camps.

1942

Feb. 26: Almost three months after Japan bombed the U.S. fleet in Pearl Harbour, 22,000 Japanese-Canadians are ordered removed from their B.C. homes and relocated to inland camps. Their houses, boats, businesses and personal property are seized.

Oct. 11: The wooden RCMP ship *St. Roch* completes the first west-to-east crossing of the Northwest Passage. The *St. Roch* is now housed in the Vancouver Maritime Museum.

Oct. 15: A hurricane kills 40,000 people in Bengal, India.

Nov. 28: Boston's Cocoanut Grove nightclub is filled to capacity when fire breaks out in the kitchen and spreads to the ballroom. The death toll is put at 491.

Dec. 12: An arson fire at the Knights of Columbus hostel in St. John's, Nfld., kills 99 people.

D-Day takes the Nazis by surprise

Operation Overlord, the Allied invasion of Normandy, sweeps over the English Channel on June 6, 1944.

Bad weather almost postpones the attack, but a decision is made to go ahead, with Canadian forces among the first into action.

RCAF Lancasters drop thousands of tons of explosives on German coastal defences; the Royal Canadian Navy provides 10,000 sailors and 109 vessels as part of the massive armada that sets out, battling choppy waters. Allied paratroopers, including 450 Canadians, jump from aircraft or land in gliders. The Canadians capture a German HQ and destroy a key bridge.

Meanwhile, Canadian soldiers in landing craft storm Juno Beach.

By the end of the day, Canadian, British and American forces have landed 155,000 troops, thousands of vehicles and hundreds of guns.

They have caught the Germans by surprise.

About 2,500 Allied soldiers are killed, including 340 Canadians.

Another 574 Canadians are wounded and 47 taken prisoner.

Operation Overlord, the biggest amphibious invasion in history, is a major turning point in the Second World War.

In an ill-planned 1942 rehearsal, 5,000 Canadians landed at Dieppe. There were 3,367 casualties, with almost 2,000 taken prisoners of war, and 907 Canadians were killed.

— National Archives

Canadian troops approach the beaches of Normandy on June 6, 1944.

THE DIONNES

WELCOME TO QUINTLAND

In 1943, a court finally returns the nine-year-old Dionne quintuplets to their family. Born in 1934, they have spent their lives being gawked at by three million visitors to "Quintland" near North Bay, Ont., across the street from the family farm.

The province of Ontario had swooped in and taken custody after word leaked out that their dad was negotiating to display them at the Chicago World's Fair.

For nine years, the five little girls have been put on display at twice-daily showings. Millions of dollars are made in endorsements, but their parents have to make appointments to see them. When the girls finally return to their family, it is like meeting strangers.

RADIO

'THIS IS MATTHEW HALTON . . .'

"Soaking wet, in a morass of mud, against an enemy fighting harder than he has fought before, the Canadians attack, attack and attack. The hillsides and farmlands and orchards are a ghastly brew of fire. Listen to the echo of those shells!"

Halton

With these words, CBC war correspondent Matthew Halton reported from the Italian frontline in December 1943. It was the first of many broadcasts that riveted Canadians with their rich descriptions of the war.

BY THE NUMBERS

1940S FACTS & FIGURES

- 11.5 million: Population of Canada after the June 11, 1941, census.
- 817,000: Population of B.C. in that census.
- 7,756: Number of immigrants arriving in Canada in 1942—the lowest since 1860.
- 7,825: Number of days William Lyon Mackenzie King held office as prime minister—to set a Canadian and Commonwealth record on Jan. 8, 1948. He eventually resigned Nov. 15 that year, adding 312 days for a grand total of 8,137—more than 22 years!

ANNE FRANK

Frank, a 14-year-old Dutch Jewish girl who kept a diary while in hiding with her family in Amsterdam, dies some time during March 1945 at the Nazi concentration camp at Bergen-Belsen.

WORLD EVENTS

CALLED TO ACCOUNT

From October 1945 to October 1946, 24 former Nazi leaders are on trial as war criminals, charged with overseeing mass murder on an unprecedented scale. The International Military Tribunal in the southern German city of Nuremberg is conducted by the victorious Allies: the United States, Britain, the Soviet Union and France. By the time punishments are meted out, one of the accused has killed himself and another has been judged incompetent. Of the remainder, three are acquitted, 12 sentenced to hang, three sentenced to life imprisonment, and four sentenced to prison terms ranging from 10 to 20 years.

POPULAR CULTURE

THE BIKINI

Louis Reard has a problem. He needs a name for his two-piece swimsuit, which he knows will be "highly explosive." In 1946, four days before unveiling his creation in Paris, the U.S. solves his problem by exploding a nuclear device near several tiny South Pacific islands known as Bikini Atoll.

BUSINESS

RISE OF GOLDEN ARCHES

"Fast food" is not yet part of the vernacular, but brothers Maurice and Richard McDonald lay the groundwork for the new industry in 1948 when they open a hamburger stand with a walk-up window in San Bernadino, Calif. In 1955, with the help of milkshake-machine salesman Ray Kroc, the brothers begin to franchise the name McDonald to entrepreneurs. McDonald's goes on to open more than 24,500 restaurants in 115 countries.

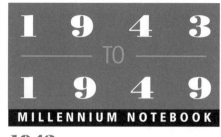

1943 TO 1949

MILLENNIUM NOTEBOOK

1943

April 19: On the feast of Passover, about 1,500 starving Jewish men and women of the Warsaw Ghetto organize into commando units and take on the German Wehrmacht armed only with pistols, grenades, Molotov cocktails, two or three light machine guns and their wits. The rebels hold out for nearly a month, killing several hundred Germans.

July 10: Canadian soldiers land in Sicily as part of the Allied invasion forces.

July 22: Trans-Canada Airlines begins the first regular non-stop flights to Britain, making the trip in 12 hours and 25 minutes. The plane is a modified Lancaster bomber and carries three passengers and armed-forces mail.

1944

Jan. 6: Bing Crosby is dethroned by a younger man known as "The Voice." Frank Sinatra becomes the new King of Croon in the annual poll conducted by *Down Beat* magazine.

June 15: The CCF wins the Saskatchewan provincial election with 44 of the 51 seats, making Rev. Tommy C. Douglas the first socialist premier in Canada.

Dec. 15: Glenn Miller, the man whose music provides a beat for the Allied march across Europe, disappears in a routine flight over the English Channel.

1945

March 18: Montreal Canadiens' Maurice (Rocket) Richard scores his 50th goal in 50 games in the final game of the season when Montreal beats Boston 4-2.

April 30: With Berlin in ruins, Adolf Hitler and Eva Braun, his wife of two days, are

holed up in a bunker beneath the German chancellery. Hitler and Braun shake hands with companions and retire to private quarters. Braun swallows cyanide and Hitler sticks a pistol into his mouth and fires. The night before, Hitler has dictated a will disclaiming responsibility for the war and blaming "international Jewry."

— National Archives

MAY 7, 1945: Dutch citizens in Utrecht welcome liberation by Canadian forces.

May 8: VE Day celebrates victory in Europe, followed by VJ Day (victory over Japan) on Aug. 14. More than a million Canadians fought in the war and 42,042 were killed.

June 20: Ottawa sends the first family allowance cheques. They will be paid to every mother for each child under age 16.

Sept. 5: Cipher clerk Igor Gouzenko defects from the Soviet Embassy in Ottawa with documents suggesting a Soviet spy ring exists in Canada.

1946

Feb. 14: ENIAC, the Electronic Numerical Integrator and Computer, is unveiled by the U.S. war department. It is three metres tall, weighs more than 27 tonnes and has 18,000 vacuum tubes.

1947

Jan. 11: Petroleum deposits are discovered in the sand banks of the Athabasca River, near Fort McMurray, Alta. Vern (Dry Hole) Hunter strikes oil near Leduc on Feb. 13, sparking an oil boom.

Atomic age ends war

With a blinding flash and a rolling grey cloud of dust that looks like an immense mushroom, a new weapon called "the atomic bomb" unleashes its fury on Hiroshima, Japan, on the morning of Aug. 6, 1945. President Harry S. Truman warns the Japanese that "if they do not accept our terms, they may expect a rain of ruin from the sky the likes of which has never been seen on this Earth." Japan does not respond. Three days later an atomic bomb falls on Nagasaki. Two cities are virtually destroyed and 120,000 people are killed outright. Japan capitulates.

The Japanese surrender on Aug. 14, following the surrender of Germany on May 8, marks the end of a six-year global conflict that left an estimated 55 million people dead. The U.S. emerges as the world's only atomic power, soon to be matched by the Soviet Union.

The new weapon is based on releasing the energy contained in the atom. It was developed in great secrecy by scientists and technicians working mostly in the remote desert of New Mexico under the direction of Army Maj.-Gen. Leslie L. Groves.

— Fort Worth Star-Telegram

July 8: A rancher brings scraps of tinfoil, paper, tape and sticks to the air base at Roswell, N.M. Lieut. Walter Haut issues a news release announcing that the base has collected remnants of a flying saucer. The scraps are rushed to Fort Worth, Texas, where Brig.-Gen. Roger M. Ramey calls a news conference identifying the scraps as debris from a weather balloon.

Aug. 14-15: At the stroke of midnight, the British Raj is replaced by the independent states of India and Pakistan. An unprecedented wave of violence kills about a million people.

Oct. 14: Reaching a speed over 1,125 km/h, U.S. Air Force Capt. Charles (Chuck) Yeager breaks the sound barrier in a Bell X-1 rocket plane he names "Glamorous Glennis" after his wife.

Nov. 20: Princess Elizabeth, daughter of Britain's King George VI, is wed to Prince Philip, the Duke of Edinburgh, in London's Westminster Abbey.

1948

Jan. 30: Mohandas Gandhi is gunned down as the 78-year-old champion of non-violence walks through a New Delhi garden to deliver a prayer to his followers. The assassin is arrested. He is Nathuran Vinayak Godse, a Hindu fanatic.

Feb. 28: The Dominion Bureau of Statistics releases a report showing that 90 per cent of Canadian homes have radios, while only 50 per cent have telephones.

May 14: A 1919 British mandate to govern Palestine expires. The new state of Israel is proclaimed, with Polish-born David Ben-Gurion as prime minister. Neighbouring Arab states invade Israel the next day and the fighting continues into 1949.

May 28: The National Party, author of apartheid, wins control of the government of South Africa. It aims to expand segregation into complete separation of the races, depriving non-whites of their rights.

Nov. 28: About 2,000 workers in Asbestos, Que., go on strike and are joined by 2,500 more at Thetford Mines. Barricades are set up and several Quebec police officers are held prisoner. A force of 400 heavily armed cops quells the strike; 180 strikers are arrested.

Dec. 14: The Supreme Court rules that the ban on margarine, in place since 1886, is illegal. The first margarine goes on sale in Vancouver on Dec. 20.

1949

Jan. 10: RCA introduces the 45-rpm record. Consumers aren't happy as it is incompatible with 78-rpm phonographs.

Jan. 15: The first non-stop coast-to-coast air flight is completed in Halifax. A Douglas DC-4 left Vancouver and flew for eight hours, 32 minutes, at 529 km/h.

March 31: Newfoundland is Canada's 10th province. Joey Smallwood is premier.

Sept. 9: A bomb aboard a Quebec Airways DC-3 explodes and the plane crashes near St. Joachim, Que.; 32 people are killed. Albert Guay is hanged for the crime in 1951.

Sept. 17: The Great Lakes excursion ship *Noronic* catches fire at a Toronto pier, killing 118.

VANCOUVER, 1940 The dial telephone doesn't come to Vancouver until 1939. The following year, at the Vancouver Exhibition at Hastings Park, residents get pointers on how to use the new device.

WEST VANCOUVER, 1946 Capt. Evan Roberts of the Royal Engineers drives the May Queen, accompanied by her attendants, to festivities at Ambleside Park in West Vancouver. Roberts is driving his precious 1935 Studebaker President convertible, bought in Victoria before the war. His daughter, *Province* reader Joan Bigford, sent us this cherished photograph.

NEW WESTMINSTER, 1940 Five-year-old Warren Bernard breaks away from mom Bernice's grip to run up to the outstretched hand of his father Jack. The British Columbia Regiment is leaving its New Westminster barracks to board a troop ship for a training camp in Nanaimo before heading overseas. The photo, by *Province* photographer Claud Detloff, is used by *Life* Magazine and hangs in Vancouver schools during the war. The youngster goes on to become mayor of Tofino and run a Chevron dealership there.

1940

The first British children evacuated for the duration of the war arrive in Vancouver.

In the first two days after the conscription of single men is announced, more than 400 marriage licences are issued in Vancouver.

The first season of Theatre Under the Stars begins in Stanley Park's Malkin Bowl. Unreserved seats are 25 cents.

Kingsway is widened to four lanes.

Vancouver's airport is reported to be the busiest in Canada, with a takeoff or landing every 81 minutes during daylight hours.

1941

West Coast shipyards begin building cargo ships to transport war supplies and food to Europe.

Gas masks go on sale to the general public.

Four of five homes in Greater Vancouver lack at least one of the following: a car, a telephone, a radio and a vacuum cleaner.

Blackout measures go into effect on the B.C. coast one day after the Japanese bomb Pearl Harbour.

Air raid sirens are tested throughout Vancouver.

1942

People of Japanese origin are forbidden to appear on public streets between dusk and dawn.

U.S. troops begin building the Alaska Highway in Peace River.

The first women workers are hired by Burrard Dry Dock in North Vancouver.

1943

Two dozen brave souls join Peter Pantages in the 22nd annual Polar Bear Swim at English Bay.

Kits beach is used for rehearsing commando beach assaults.

1944

Prefabricated houses arrive. Homes sell for $3,600 each.

The RCMP ship *St. Roch* arrives in Vancouver from Halifax via the Northwest Passage. The trip takes 86 days. The ship made the first west-east crossing in 1942.

KELOWNA, 1948 Adolph Roth stands beside the van he uses to deliver Kelowna Creamery products door-to-door in Kelowna. Roth has been in Kelowna since 1927, first delivering milk by horse and wagon. In this photo, submitted by *Province* reader Violetta Roth of Vancouver, it's interesting to note the two-digit phone number on the van door.

— Cowichan Valley Museum 996.1.2.5

— Canadian Press

DUNCAN, 1942 An anti-aircraft gun is installed behind the Duncan armouries to defend against sudden attack by the Japanese. "Whether you like it or not, I am here to tell you that you are going to be bombed this year," B.C.'s assistant provincial fire marshall tells an audience of firefighters and emergency workers at a school gym in Duncan. Ever since Japan's attack on the U.S. Navy base at Pearl Harbor on Dec. 7, 1941, B.C. has been on alert.

— Pacific Press Library

Opposite: **HATZIC, 1948** When heavy snowpack turns the Fraser River into a wall of water, it flows over its banks and floods about 22,000 hectares of the Fraser Valley. More than 16,000 residents are driven to higher ground and watch helplessly as their homes are flooded or washed away. This school in Hatzic is almost up to its eaves on June 29, 1948. Sandbagging and damage repairs cost $20 million. The flood leads to $160 million being spent on new dikes.

VANCOUVER, 1942 Japanese-Canadians say their goodbyes at a Vancouver train station. About 22,000 are sent to internment camps in the Interior and across Canada after being rounded up and stripped of their homes, fishboats and possessions.

1944 continued:

Students with summer jobs in war industries get more pay than their teachers, prompting teachers in Surrey to seek a raise.

1945

The first double chairlift in North America is built on Grouse Mountain.

The first Cloverdale Rodeo takes place.

Victoria-born painter and author Emily Carr dies at 73.

The first family allowance cheques arrive in the mail. The allowance is $5 a month for a child under six and $59 for five or more children.

Ads of the day: Teacher wanted for Cumberland High School, salary $1,600 per year; small poultry farm and hatchery in Richmond, 2 acres, includes three-room bungalow and 350 chickens, $5,300; solitaire diamond ring, $35 at Shore's Jeweller.

1946

In Cloverdale and White Rock, 264 people are on waiting lists for phones.

The biggest earthquake to hit B.C. in the past century rattles the coast on June 23. The 7.3-Richter quake hits Vancouver Island hardest.

1947

Parking meters arrive in B.C.

The last streetcar retires from service in North Vancouver.

The worst polio outbreak in 20 years prompts the closure of wading pools.

1948

The first TV signal reaches Vancouver with broadcasts from Seattle.

Sixty thousand daffodil bulbs—a gift from Holland to thank Canadian soldiers for helping liberate their country—are planted along the Stanley Park Causeway.

1949

Expansion of the Pacific Great Eastern Railway from Quesnel to Prince George goes ahead after being halted in the early '20s.

Kingsway reopens as a six-lane highway between Vancouver and New Westminster.

Japanese and aboriginals are given the right to vote in B.C. provincial elections.

–Hardip Johal

WEST VANCOUVER, 1943 With men away at war, women join the civil defence program as Air Raid Protection volunteers. This group of wardens has signed on for the West Vancouver auxiliary firefighting unit. Altogether, about 10,000 B.C. residents signed on for ARP duties during the Second World War.

— The Province

— The Province

VANCOUVER, 1945 Vancouver residents flock to the streets to celebrate VJ-Day, the day the Japanese surrender, on Aug. 14, 1945. Traffic clogs the downtown as people form conga lines, dance, cheer, wave flags and throw streamers. It is the beginning of a new era of peace, and heralds the return of Canadian troops from overseas.

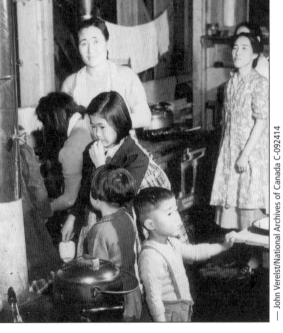

— John Verelst/National Archives of Canada C-092414

GREENWOOD, 1943 Japanese families gather in a community kitchen at an Interior internment camp at Greenwood, B.C. Families have arrived in open trucks at the camps with a few belongings. They live in wooden shacks, heated by wood stoves. They spend the rest of the war there, farming and eking out an existence. Many never return to the coast, where they were born and where their families had prosperous businesses until they were forced to give up everything.

Salt of the earth

Sir—

When *HMS Implacable,* the huge British aircraft carrier, loomed into sight at Prospect Point on Thursday morning, a man made the remark to his friend: "I suppose that we shall hear nothing but what the British Navy did for the next few days."

Two American soldiers standing near said: "You can thank God if you do hear it. They saved you and us as well. They are the salt of the earth."

This put on the finishing touch.

BRITISHER
Vancouver, Oct. 15, 1945

The British aircraft carrier *HMS Implacable* docks in Vancouver harbour in 1945.

—Vancouver Public Library, Special Collections 68790

Work for older women

Sir—

I wish to protest against the employment of married women who already have husbands earning for them. There are far too many such cases.

This is not fair to women who have to earn their own living. I am a 58-year-old widow and the only work I am offered is the hardest housework which, at my age, I cannot hold long enough to earn my living.

If the strong and younger married women are not satisfied with their husbands' wages, let them do the housework. Let the older women and others who have to earn a living have those easier jobs, which they could hold and from which they could make a decent living.

Human need before human greed.

CONSTANT READER
Vancouver, Nov. 5, 1945

Pupils become boorish

Sir—

We are going to spend $4 million to increase the efficiency of our school system. It would be nice if part of this could be used to educate our teachers so they could infuse into their pupils a little bit of old-fashioned courtesy.

This development in boorish manners among our young people has become apparent in the last 15 years.

CANADIAN
Vancouver, Nov. 5, 1945

Bear the noise

Sir—

Two anonymous correspondents object to noise of planes passing over their houses. Evidently they are willing to accept the benefits of peace and security from the war, but not the smallest personal inconvenience. Have they ever given a thought to the deadly V-bombs disturbing Britain or the inferno of noise our boys at the front must sleep through?

I, too, live in a district used day and night for plane practice and am sometimes wakened by a low-flying machine just long enough to feel thankful it is not Jap or German and to wish the best of luck to the men up there in the cold and darkness.

J.I. CROFT
Cloverdale, March 3, 1945

Five years in Europe

Sir—

I enclose a few excerpts from a letter from my son who was in the Sicilian and Italian campaigns and is now in northwestern Europe. He has been overseas since January 1940. He is a married man. Has he not done enough?

"I can't say when I'll be on the home leave scheme. Like a lot more, we've quit thinking of it, and only plan on our trip back, when the war is finished.

"What we have read and seen of our reinforcement scheme from Canada has only disgusted us. It has taken the people of Canada a long time to become alive to the true situation. We hope now they will make a push in the right direction. Personally I would rather rot here than take my trip back and know I had to come back at the end of 30 days.

"It seems all that is necessary is to tell us some reinforcements are on the way. We have done our part but a lot more could be done in other places."

DISGUSTED MOTHER OF FOUR INTHE SERVICES
Enderby, April 7, 1945

Vancouver's disgrace

Sir —

Miss Dawn Bohmer has voiced her opinion on the banning of unescorted girls in dance halls.

The percentage of VD (venereal disease) in this city is disgusting. I have just been discharged from the Air Force, and in my travels I haven't found one city across Canada that has the same trouble with VD as Vancouver.

The place to start cleaning this city of its VD is the street corners—the number of young girls hanging around Smithe and Granville is alarming.

The blame should not fall on the unescorted women going into dance halls, most of whom are out just for a pleasant evening.

HERBERT PATTISON
Vancouver, Dec. 17, 1945

Old-fashioned remedies

Sir —

As there are so many children away from schools sick just now, I send two useful hints. The first is a remedy for whooping cough. It is inexpensive, easy to make, effective and pleasant to take. Boil half a pint of malt vinegar with a clove of bruised garlic. When it boils, strain it and stir in half a pint of molasses. Give a tablespoon occasionally.

To keep germs from spreading, keep a medium-sized open saucepan on the stove simmering filled with water and a table-

CBC broadcasts

Sir—

When our radio tax was raised to $2, the Radio Commission assured radio owners they would not be inflicted with advertising; and what are we getting? More and more advertising—mostly for soap.

Until this week we had a delightful program of good and bright music from 8:15 to 9 a.m. This has been changed to a sort of vaudeville program advertising butter. It is awful tripe and is punctuated by studio applause which makes listening impossible, if one wished to waste the time.

Again at 9:15 a.m. there is a program called "Big Sister," which has been going on for months, and which must have a very unwholesome influence on its listeners. Most of the characters are morons and extraordinarily unpleasant. I'm surprised the women's clubs have not made a protest.

I have another strenuous protest to make, and this is in reference to the vaudeville program from 6:30 to 7 p.m. It is a skit on rehabilitation committees. My husband and self thought it was in execrable taste, making fun of men who are giving up leisure hours to the important job of helping our servicemen back to civil life.

One wonders at the mentality of the CBC staff. I am sure there are others who hope as I do that something will be done. After all, we pay their salaries.

G. GRAY
West Vancouver, Oct. 15, 1945

spoon of Condy's fluid (one ounce of permanganate of potash with one gallon of water). Also useful as a mouth wash or gargle and is excellent for relieving hot or tired feet.

OLD-FASHIONED HOUSEWIFE
Cloverdale, May 3, 1945

People want election

Sir —

Mackenzie King's excuses for avoiding an election are as implausible as his voice is unconvincing.

Contrary to his contention that the Grey North byelection shows Canadians do not desire a general election during wartime, Grey North proved that Mr. King's government no longer represents the people of Canada.

There is not the slightest doubt that the government's disallowance of the general election now due is based firstly on a determination to retain office. Mr. King's prattlings about servicemen's opinions are exactly opposite to those of the men from the battlefront with whom I have very recently talked.

V.O.V.
Courtenay, March 28, 1945

— Vancouver Public Library, Special Collections 62485

Vancouver International Airport, 1953

At the height of her career, Hollywood superstar Marilyn Monroe lands in Vancouver en route to Los Angeles, taking time to vamp for the cameras beneath the tail of a DC-6. Monroe has just finished filming River of No Return with Robert Mitchum in Banff (the movie is released the following year) and is on her way home to L.A. In 1953, Monroe and Jane Russell can be seen co-starring on the silver screen in the musical comedy *Gentlemen Prefer Blondes.*

B.C. TAKES OFF

BY DAMIAN INWOOD

A s we reach the mid-way point in the century, it's a time for unprecedented expansion in B.C.

The Aluminum Company of Canada takes the lead, building a new plant at Kitimat on a remote northwest inlet.

Starting in 1951, Alcan spends three years building a new city of 13,500 people in virgin forest.

The following year sees the politically savvy W.A.C. Bennett start his 20-year reign as Social Credit premier of B.C.

With his lieutenant, highways minister "Flying Phil" Gagliardi, he launches a policy of road-building that eventually sees every significant town linked by blacktop.

On the world stage, the Korean War is well under way, with a contingent of Canadians going to fight alongside the U.S.

In the South Pacific, nuclear tests are becoming commonplace and the giant mushroom cloud becomes a symbol of 20th century Armageddon.

Canada has a new Queen. She is Elizabeth II, eldest daughter of George VI, and she is crowned in 1953.

The Empire Games come to Vancouver in 1954 and crowds witness "the Miracle Mile" on Aug. 7. Two men, Roger Bannister from Britain and Australian John Landy, run the

mile in under four minutes. Bannister beats Landy and a statue is later erected, freezing in time the moment when Landy looks over one shoulder while Bannister passes him on the other side.

Empire Stadium witnesses another event that leaves people divided on its merits.

Elvis Presley plays there Aug. 31, 1957, and 22,000 fans are on hand. Some end up fighting with police after Elvis sings just five songs and leaves the building.

Province music critic Dr. Ida Halpern likens Presley's gyrations to "the convulsions of a frog injected with strychnine, with its legs shivering and jittering."

In 1957, The Wham-O Company introduces the Frisbee. In 1959 it will unveil the Hula Hoop and will sell 25 million of them in four months.

Burrard Inlet is hit by tragedy on June 17, 1958, when the Second Narrows Bridge collapses killing 18 steelworkers.

In October 1959, swashbuckling screen star Errol Flynn, 50, dies of a heart attack in a West End Vancouver penthouse.

As the '50s end, we still live in a world of innocence filled with drive-ins, sock hops and big-finned cars.

The next decade is destined to present a much more cynical scenario.

> Canada has a new Queen. She is Elizabeth II, eldest daughter of George VI, and she is crowned in 1953

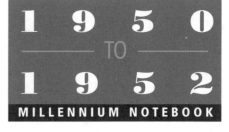

1950

Jan. 19: The RCAF-designed Avro CF-100 jet fighter flies for the first time. The long-range, radar-equipped jet will be replaced by the Avro CF-105 in 1958.

Jan. 31: President Harry S. Truman orders the U.S. Atomic Energy Commission to begin developing a hydrogen bomb.

Feb. 9: A U.S. senator claims that communist agents have infiltrated the government. Sen. Joseph McCarthy, R-Wis., holds hearings to prove his allegations and "McCarthyism" becomes a household word. A Senate panel in July concludes that his accusations have no foundation.

April 25: B.C., Alberta, Saskatchewan, Manitoba, Ontario and Prince Edward Island sign an agreement to create the Trans-Canada Highway. Work begins in the summer and ends in 1970.

May 5: The Red River in Manitoba floods its banks and forces 100,000 from their homes. Soldiers and volunteers build dikes.

Hollywood movie star Elizabeth Taylor marries hotel heir Nick Hilton. Her former nanny says: "Elizabeth loves and respects Mr. Hilton. He feels the same about her. That's why this will be the first and last marriage for both of them."

May 29: The RCMP ship *St. Roch* becomes the first vessel to circumnavigate North America.

June 25: The Korean War begins; 25,000 Canadian troops will participate as part of a UN force. By war's end, July 27, 1953, 314 Canadians will be killed and 1,211 wounded.

Sept. 15: UN forces launch a massive invasion at Inchon, South Korea. Fierce fighting continues, with UN forces liberating Seoul on Sept. 26 and reaching the North's capital, Pyongyang, a month later.

Oct. 2: The United Feature Syndicate begins distributing the comic *Peanuts*, by Charles Schulz.

1951

June 25: The first colour TV broadcast is presented by CBS. Unfortunately, only

On-the-fly recording launches The King

July 5, 1954, marks a turning point in the life of a 19-year-old truck driver in Memphis, Tenn. Elvis Aron Presley, an aspiring entertainer from Tupelo, Miss., brings his guitar to Sun Studios, where owner Sam Phillips has finally agreed to allow him a real recording session. Earlier, Presley paid Phillips $4 to make a "vanity" record.

Presley is joined by two seasoned pros, guitarist Scotty Moore and bass player Bill Black, for a practice session on July 4; the next day, the trio goes to work on Presley's idea for an up-tempo version of a blues tune—"That's All Right", by Arthur (Big Boy) Crudup. After several takes, the trio finds a tempo and blend that seems to work. The recording launches the Elvis phenomenon, thanks to a boost by Memphis disc jockey Dewey Phillips. The DJ, no relation to Sam Phillips, is deluged with phone calls after playing the record only once.

Just 25 days later, Presley, Moore and Black play a concert in Memphis. Presley fails to control a nervous twitch in his leg. As he will later recall: "I came offstage and my manager told me that they was hollering because I was wiggling my legs. I went back out for an encore and I did a little more. And the more I did, the wilder they went."

Elizabeth a queen at 25

Princess Elizabeth and her husband, Prince Philip, are in the first week of what is intended to be a five-month goodwill tour of East Africa, where they are lodged at Treetops on the night of Feb. 5-6, 1952. During the night, as Elizabeth sleeps in Kenya and her father, King George VI, slumbers at the royal estate of Sandringham in England, the king dies peacefully of advanced lung cancer and heart disease.

Unaware that the British crown has passed to her during the night, Elizabeth sets out at dawn to fish for trout. Not until lunchtime does the news reach the angling party that George VI is dead. Suddenly, it dawns on this 25-year-old woman, who until now has led a carefree life, that she is queen.

The eldest daughter of George VI, Elizabeth Alexandra Mary takes the oath of accession to the British throne on Feb. 8 and is proclaimed head of the British Commonwealth. She will be formally crowned in Westminster Abbey on June 2, 1953.

CBS technicians can see it; no colour TV sets are owned by the public.

Oct. 15: *I Love Lucy*, starring redheaded comedienne Lucille Ball, makes its premiere on CBS.

1952

Jan. 24: Vincent Massey becomes the first Canadian-born Governor General of Canada.

Mar. 8: A mechanical heart is placed for the first time in a human by surgeons at the Pennsylvania Hospital in Philadelphia. The patient dies 81 hours later.

July 7: The liner *SS United States* sets a trans-Atlantic speed record on its first trip to Europe with an eastward crossing of three days, 10 hours and 40 minutes.

Aug. 30: Inventor R. Buckminster Fuller displays a strong, lightweight structure called a "geodesic dome." The dome revolutionizes construction techniques.

Sept. 6: Canada's first television station, CBFT, begins broadcasting in Montreal. Then the English-language CBFT begins its broadcasts in Toronto Sept. 8.

Nov. 1: The U.S. Atomic Energy Commission explodes the first hydrogen bomb, at the Eniwetok proving grounds in the Pacific Ocean. The explosion is 500 times more powerful than the bomb that destroyed Hiroshima in 1945.

MAGAZINES

SEX SELLS

Hugh Hefner, 27, sets off fireworks in the magazine industry with the first issue of *Playboy* in 1953. It features Marilyn Monroe on the cover and as the model in the centrefold.

Hefner

The first issue has no date because Hefner isn't sure there will be a second. The new magazine—built around the centrefold, includes some serious journalism, fiction and advice to its young, upwardly mobile readers about how to live the good life.

It proves so successful that it is soon outselling the reigning men's magazine, *Esquire*, for which Hefner once worked.

TECHNOLOGY

THE TUBE PROLIFERATES

TV is rapidly displacing radio as a source of family entertainment and, by 1951, a few thousand Lower Mainland homes have rooftop aerials. At first, they can receive only fuzzy pictures from Washington State—the coronation of Queen Elizabeth II in June

1953 is carried by Bellingham's KVOS. CBC's local station, CBUT, goes on the air in December 1953, a year after National Hockey League games are first shown on Canadian TV. By now, 10 per cent of Canadian households have a TV. Newscasts on the English and French networks begin in 1954 and CBC is the host broadcaster for the British Empire Games. From the U.S. come shows like *Hopalong Cassidy* and *American Bandstand*, which is hosted by a 22-year-old named Dick Clark.

AHHHHHH, COOL AIR

General Motors announces that it will offer air-conditioning as an option in some of its 1953 car models. Tests in Texas and Arizona show that the systems can reduce the heat of a car to a comfortable level within minutes, no matter how long the vehicle has been in the sun.

ICONS

Shapely, wrinkle-free, with pouty lips and impossible measurements, Barbie is born March 9, 1959. The fashion doll that will make generations of young girls feel inadequate about their bodies is the plastic offspring of Mattel founders Ruth and Elliot Handler. She is named for their daughter, Barbara. The doll's debut takes place at the American Toy Fair in New York.

DISNEY'S DREAM

1955 is a banner year for Walt. The TV show *Disneyland* is high in the ratings. The Mickey Mouse Club becomes a must-see for kids. And a Disneyland theme park opens July 17 in Anaheim, Calif.

ROSA'S RIDE

Seamstress Rosa Parks, 43, refuses to give up her seat near the front of a city bus on Dec. 1, 1955, in Montgomery, Ala. For this she is arrested and fined $10. But her simple act of defiance leads to a U.S. Supreme Court ruling in 1956 that bus segregation is illegal.

BOOKS

THE BEAT GENERATION

With publication of his novel *On the Road* in '57, Jack Kerouac becomes the spokesman for the restless, disaffected Beat Generation.

OTHER POPULAR READS OF THE '50S:

- *The Cat in the Hat,* by Dr. Seuss, aims at beginning readers bored with dull old Dick and Jane.
- *On the Beach,* by Nevil Shute.

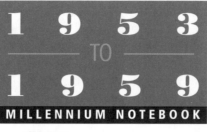

1953 TO 1959
MILLENNIUM NOTEBOOK

1953

March 5: Josef Stalin, the most brutal leader in Russia's history, dies in Moscow at age 73. His handpicked heir, Georgi Malenkov, 51, assumes control of the U.S.S.R. Nikita Khrushchev, 58, emerges as second-in-command. In 1958, he takes control.

May 29: Mountaineer Edmund Hillary of New Zealand and Tenzing Norgay, his Nepalese Sherpa guide, become the first men to conquer Mount Everest.

July 13: The Stratford Festival opens in Stratford, Ont., in a tent theatre. The first production is *Richard III,* with Alec Guinness.

Sept. 12: Sen. John F. Kennedy weds Jacqueline Bouvier in Newport, R.I..

1954

March 30: Canada's first subway line opens in Toronto.

May 6: Briton Roger Bannister runs the mile in just under four minutes. Six weeks later, Australian John Landy runs it in 3:58. Bannister later beats Landy in the "Miracle Mile" in Vancouver.

Oct. 15: Hurricane Hazel, the worst storm in Canadian history, reaches Toronto and causes 83 deaths and significant property damage.

Oct. 10: The groundbreaking ceremony for the St. Lawrence Seaway is held at Cornwall, Ont. and Massena, N.Y.

1955

April 12: U.S. microbiologist Jonas Salk announces that his vaccine for polio is safe. Salk refuses to patent the vaccine, saying he has no wish to profit from it.

June 11: Eighty people die and nearly 100 are injured as the worst accident in the history of auto racing occurs at Le Mans, France. Three cars are involved and one slams into a grandstand.

Sept. 30: Movie star James Dean, 24, dies when his Porsche skids off a California road and smashes into a telephone pole.

Four days later, Warner Bros. releases *Rebel Without a Cause.*

1956

April 19: Grace Kelly, at the pinnacle of her movie career, marries Monaco's Prince Rainier III.

June 29: Actress Marilyn Monroe and playwright Arthur Miller marry, she for the third time, he for the second.

June 30: In the worst commercial air disaster to date, 128 die when two airliners crash into the Grand Canyon.

July 25: At 11:10 p.m., about 100 kilometres off Nantucket Island, the Italian liner *Andrea Doria* and Swedish liner *Stockholm* collide in fog. During the next 11 hours, before the *Andrea Doria* slides beneath the sea, people gather around TVs and radios to follow the plight of the stricken liners. Fifty-one people die.

July 26: Egypt's nationalist president, Gamal Abdel Nasser, seizes the Suez Canal from the French-controlled Suez Canal Co. The action makes Nasser an Arab hero. Israel invades the Sinai Peninsula and the Gaza Strip Oct. 29, followed by a French-British invasion of Egypt on Oct. 31. All troops will be gone by spring 1957.

Sept. 24: The world's first trans-Atlantic telephone cable begins operation. The twin cables, 3,620 km long, stretch from Newfoundland, to Oban, Scotland.

Oct. 23: Protesting Budapest students demand free speech and free elections in Hungary. They are suppressed when Soviet tanks roll in on Nov. 4. More than 37,000 refugees flee to Canada.

Nov. 1: A mine accident at Springhill, N.S., kills 39 men and 88 miners are trapped but are later rescued.

Dec. 9: A DC-4 airliner crashes into Slesse Mountain in B.C., killing all 62 people aboard.

1957

March 25: The European Economic Community is created as Belgium, France, West Germany, Italy, Luxembourg and the Netherlands sign the Treaty of Rome.

Sept. 4: Arkansas National Guardsmen turn away nine black students enrolled at Central High School in Little Rock, Ark. The "Little Rock Nine" return to school Sept. 23 but are sent home when rioting whites overwhelm police. On Sept. 25, armed troops escort the black students to class.

Beeps from the sky

The launch of the *Sputnik* started the Cold War space race.

— Knight Ridder

For the first time in human history, an artificial satellite is dispatched Oct. 4, 1957, to orbit the Earth. The 84-kilogram aluminum sphere, smaller than a basketball, circles the globe every 95 minutes, emitting ominous "beeps" and transmitting data to its masters on terra firma. Trouble is, those masters are in the Soviet Union. And that causes no end of worry for Americans in the paranoid Cold War world. Humankind has made a first tentative step into the cosmos, and the space race between the world's two superpowers is off and running.

As *Sputnik* circles the globe, astronomers rush to track its orbit and eavesdrop on its radio signal, politicians stake out positions, and U.S. President Dwight Eisenhower dismisses it as "one small ball in the air, something that does not raise my apprehension, not one iota." But Sen. Stuart Symington of Missouri sums up the worries of many Americans on Oct. 5: "Unless our defence policies are promptly changed, the Soviets will move from superiority to supremacy."

Oct. 14: Lester B. Pearson is awarded the Nobel Peace Prize for his work on the Suez Crisis and for organizing an international peace force.

1958
Mar. 25: The new *Avro Arrow*, the CF-105, breaks the sound barrier in its first test flight in Ontario. On Feb. 20, 1959, Prime Minister John Diefenbaker will shock the aircraft industry by cancelling the *Avro* project, stating that manned bombers will not be a threat to North America. He also cites prohibitive development costs due to U.S. refusal to buy the aircraft.

May 23: Dissatisfied with his country's standing in the economic world order, Mao Tse-tung launches China on a "Great Leap Forward."

Millions of peasants are organized into about 24,000 "people's communes" in the countryside. Historians will later estimate that 20 million or more Chinese died in the resulting famine.

June 17: Vancouver's Second Narrows Bridge collapses during construction, killing 18 men.

June 28: Pele leads Brazil to the World Cup soccer title with a 5-2 win over Sweden.

Oct. 23: A tunnel collapses in the Springhill, N.S., mine, killing 74. This is the third accident to take lives at this mine.

Oct. 26: The jet age dawns when Pan American World Airways launches trans-Atlantic flights between New York and Paris using a Boeing 707.

Oct. 28: Angelo Giuseppe Cardinal Roncali, patriarch of Venice, is named pope to succeed Pius XII, who died Oct. 9. The new pope will be known as John XXIII.

1959
Jan. 1: Led by a fiery 32-year-old lawyer named Fidel Castro, rebels seize power in Cuba after two years of civil war. Dictator Fulgencio Batista resigns after seven years in power and flees to Miami.

Feb. 3: A four-seater plane carrying touring performers Ritchie Valens, J.P. (The Big Bopper) Richardson and Buddy Holly takes off after 1 a.m en route to Fargo, N.D. A few kilometres from the airport, it plunges into a snow-covered cornfield in Iowa, killing all three.

Nov. 18: The Board of Broadcast Governors creates the first Canadian-content rules for TV.

A crowd flocks around Canada's *Avro Arrow* CF-105 in 1958.

— Canadian Press

POLIO VACCINATIONS, 1955 In this photograph taken in April of 1955, schoolboys line up to be vaccinated against polio. Several poliomyelitis epidemics hit Canada from 1929 to 1948, but the most serious outbreak occurs in 1952-53, when record numbers are afflicted. The polio threat subsides after April 12, 1954, when a vaccine developed by Jonas Salk of the University of Pittsburgh is declared safe and effective against the terrifying disease. The public reaction to the vaccine is emotional and jubilant, an expression you can't quite see on the faces of these lads as they steel themselves against the needle's point.

DELTA DRIVE-IN, 1953 Mobile moviegoers prepare for dusk at the new Delta Drive-In, which opens in May of '53. (A decade later, there are 44 drive-in theatres around B.C.; today there are fewer than a handful.) Before the onslaught of television, the shopping-mall cinema and later the video cassette, the drive-in theatre is an integral part of growing up. During its heyday, the Delta Drive-In entertains hundreds of thousands of customers a year and hosts flea-market garage sales on Sunday mornings; today, it is a mixed residential development.

— Vancouver Public Library, Special Collections 41563

— Vancouver Public Library, Special Collections 45953-A

— Vancouver Public Library, Special Collections 81522

INTERNATIONAL CINEMA, 1951

Katharine Hepburn, then 41, makes her first personal and public appearance in Vancouver in the early days of 1951. Here the Hollywood star accepts a small totem pole from an unidentified man, presumably a representative of the International Cinema theatre where Hepburn stars as Rosalind in Shakespeare's *As You Like It* from Jan. 31 to Feb. 3. The show, co-starring William Prince, is a critical success and sells out each night. Three months later, Hepburn is en route to Africa to film *The African Queen* with Humphrey Bogart and director John Huston.

EMPIRE STADIUM, 1957

Police and security guards form a human chain in a vain attempt to keep teenage fans under control as Elvis Presley prepares to shake his booty for 22,000 fans at Empire Stadium. The Aug. 31 show (tickets are $2) lasts just 35 minutes. Youths repeatedly charge the police line protecting the stage as The King rocks them into a frenzy. The screaming hysteria and ensuing melee is something entirely new to Vancouver in 1957 and, according to the scribes of the day, a frightening sight to behold.

—Vancouver Public Library, Special Collections 61267

SEYMOUR NARROWS, OFF CAMPBELL RIVER, 1958

Ka-boom! One of the biggest non-nuclear explosions in history takes out Ripple Rock in Seymour Narrows. The hazard to navigation on Canada's route to Alaska—one of the rock's two peaks is just three metres below the surface—is obliterated with 1.25 million kilograms of nitromex 2H. (In 1945, there was actually some discussion among scientists and politicians about blasting the rock to bits with an atomic bomb.)

— B.C. Archives D-08490

SEMIAHMOO PARK, 1950s Not exactly a picture postcard for supernatural B.C., this scene of weekend leisure circa 1950s shows families camping in canvas tents adjacent to the railway tracks and power lines on the edge of Semiahmoo Park. During the '50s the park is a popular weekend getaway for families. Adjacent to Semiahmoo Park is a sandy-bottomed bay with warm, shallow waters, an ideal spot for a summer dip.

— City of Surrey Archives 150.01

— B.C. Archives H-05656

INTERIOR PEACE COAL MINES, 1950 Although it looks like it dates from a much earlier era, this picture of a miner and his horse at work in the Interior Peace Coal Mines in northeastern B.C. was actually taken in 1950. It is probably among the last pieces of evidence of horses being used to move ore in B.C. mines. Neither man nor beast looks particularly pleased as they glare into the camera lens.

1955

Canadian Pacific Airlines begins service between Vancouver and Amsterdam over the North Pole. It takes 18 hours to complete the 7,800-kilometre trip.

Vancouver hosts its first Grey Cup.

The provincial government buys Lions Gate Bridge for $6 million, half its appraised value.

1956

Stanley Park Aquarium opens and goes on to become North America's third largest aquarium.

The new Homeowner's Grant gives homeowners in B.C. $28 a year.

Red Robinson emcees Vancouver's first rock and roll concert. Bill Haley and the Comets perform for 6,000 at Kerrisdale Arena.

The Black Ball Ferry Co. makes its first run to Bowen Island.

1957

The new main branch of the Vancouver Public Library opens at the corner of Robson and Burrard.

The Oak Street Bridge opens.

1958

Prompted by labour disputes that disrupted private ferry service, Premier W.A.C. Bennett announces B.C. will launch its own ferry fleet.

Shaughnessy Golf Course signs a long-term lease with the Department of Indian Affairs for part of the Musqueam Indian reserve on southwest Marine Drive.

The PNE grounds become home to the largest roller coaster in Canada.

1959

The first car travels through the Deas Island Tunnel in May.

The last execution in B.C. takes place with the hanging of Leo Mantha.

Matinee idol Errol Flynn dies in Vancouver.

–Hardip Johal

KEMANO DAM, 1953
Hard rock miners and their equipment are dwarfed by the vastness of the powerhouse cavern at Kemano, which could easily accommodate the Hotel Vancouver upon completion. This Aug. 31 picture shows the cavern before excavations were made in the floor for turbines which would produce electricity for smelting aluminum in Kitimat, an industry that gave the town life later in '53. Miners blasted through 16 kilometres and 2,300,000 tonnes of rock in 21 months to complete the Alcan project, breaking speed and volume records in the process.

— The Province

VANCOUVER, 1958 The Second Narrows Bridge collapses on June 17, 1958, midway through construction. Eighteen workmen are killed and another 20 are injured after the north anchor arm gives way. This photograph, taken the day after the collapse, shows rescue workers searching through the twisted, broken metal for victims of the tragedy. The Second Narrows, with a cantilevered main span of 350 metres, is completed in 1960. In 1995 the bridge is officially renamed the Ironworkers Memorial Second Narrows Crossing in honour of the victims who died in the collapse.

— The Province

— Vancouver Public Library, Special Collections 60820

It wasn't until 1958 that Howie Goss (above, pictured at Capilano Stadium) and his fellow Vancouver Mounties were able to play legally on a Sunday. The 10-year struggle over Sunday sport in Vancouver went all the way to the Supreme Court of Canada.

'Blind stupidity' on sport

Sir —

The blind stupidity of the city council on the issue of Sunday sports is beyond comprehension.

The advent of Coast League baseball in Vancouver is really an event of great importance—even more significant than the coming of professional football. Coast League baseball means that Vancouver is really big-time in sports. Vancouver's population and progressive spirit justify such a status.

The city council is to be commended for authorizing improvements at Capilano Stadium. But what does it do then?

It virtually slams the door against the prospect of making this investment pay off as it should by arrogantly refusing citizens the right to vote on whether they approve of Sunday sport. Everyone knows that Sunday double-headers are the big attraction in baseball, the best guarantee of keeping a league franchise in sound financial condition. And Sunday baseball need not interfere with church-going.

Sunday sport will eventually come to Vancouver, just as it has come to Montreal and Toronto and will probably come to Winnipeg after next week's vote.

But our backward-looking council, evidently afraid of some puritanical bogy, drags its feet. Let's hope that we keep Vancouver in the Coast League. If we don't, we'll know who's to blame.

GEORGE A. SMITH
Vancouver, Oct. 18, 1955

East Side neglected

Sir —

After reading Ald. Sprott's remarks regarding Fire Chief Bird's decision to "fire" the Inhalator Squad in the Kerrisdale district, I felt that we in the East End have at last got a break.

It was indeed a revelation to hear that five of the eight aldermen on the City Council reside in the Kerrisdale district. Now we know why the East End is ALWAYS like a cow's tail in the matter of civic development. Who is the last to get ornamental lighting? Hastings East. Who is the last to get the streetcar lines torn up? Hastings East. Who is the last to get the dial telephones? Hastings East. Who pays their taxes on time in preference to keeping up with the Joneses? Hastings East.

Nice figuring Chief Bird.

This should be a warning to civic electors next December. Make sure that YOUR district is going to have representation in the next council, regardless of political party . . .

Electors in Hastings East do NOT let this happen again.

C.E.W. RUMBALL,
Vancouver, May 17, 1955

No Arabs!

Sir —

At the meeting of the Independent Association of Orangemen, a non-political body, the following letter was read and unanimously endorsed: That whereas it has been ascertained that our Canadian Government is in favour of displaced Palestine Arabs being emigrated to this country, and whereas a former government was responsible for placing the Doukhobors here with a great expense to this province, so we raise the battle cry: "No Arabs For Canada!" And if our government insists then take them to their beloved Quebec. But no Palestine Arabs for British Columbia.

JOHN RUDDOCK
Independent Assn. of Orangemen,
Dec. 10, 1955

Unimpressed by bridge

Sir —

Recently a prominent bridge builder passed through Vancouver and I was in a position to speak to him in regard to his opinion of the Granville Bridge, and future bridges that are going to be built here.

It might be of interest for us to know, now that a big bridge-building program has started, what an outstanding engineer thinks of our bridge-building technique in Western Canada. He mentioned first of all that he was surprised at the somewhat strange location of the bridge, as such, when it would have been much more advantageous to fill in False Creek, and thereby more cheaply provide the public with all the needed through streets.

In regard to the design of the bridge, he felt that approximately three times more steel than needed had been used. He said that the concrete surfacing of the bridge is the poorest job he has seen anywhere in the world ...

He concluded that the bridge had cost the taxpayer twice as much money as would be deemed necessary.

HARRY PEDERSEN
Vancouver, June 8, 1955

Seattle the Good

Sir—

Spending three days in Seattle on the Easter weekend proved refreshing because I did not see any drunks.

In Vancouver, any day after noon one sees drunken men and women lounging about the streets, which is disgusting, and at 11:30 p.m. when beer parlours "spew" out their patrons, it is even worse. If police are enforcing regulations, what is the reason for this drunkenness?

Instead of "licensed premises" and "ladies" and "gentlemen" every few yards on the main streets, which reminds one of a toilet, one sees in Seattle original names such as Bob's Tavern, Sunset Tavern, Last Chance, and others in colourful neon lights.

Seattle is the cleanest city in which I have ever lived or visited. The contrast with Vancouver is striking at every turn.

This, however, is not the fault of the city but of the people, for daily on downtown streets and in residential districts alike one sees men throw the empty cigarette package on the sidewalk after they have taken the last cigarette, although there is a trash can a few yards distant.

A REALIST,
Vancouver, April 22, 1955

Butter and health

Sir —

One crusade you should continue – cheaper butter. It is indeed scandalous that Canadians should be compelled to pay such high prices for butter when apparently a country such as Czechoslovakia will be obtaining Canadian butter at much reduced prices.

Milk and politics

Sir —

It seems, in these days, there is always a committee investigating milk. Why milk? Milk is a necessity for children but so are fruit, vegetables and many other things which never get investigated.

Stranger still is the fact that milk is controlled by government officials and when it is controlled, where can there be any exploitation? B.C. newspapers have been carrying the statistics of our milk hearings. The idea seems that the farmer should receive his guaranteed price, the consumer cheaper milk. What about the people in the middle? Is the dairy worker to have a living wage?

At present the driver receives no statutory holidays. Are there many people who receive no statutory holidays? They also have no set hours of work. If a driver's truck breaks down or he is delayed for any one of many reasons, he receives no overtime. This is just part of his day's work. Compare the dairy worker to the labourer who receives $1.60 per hour: The dairy worker receives the monthly equivalent of $1.40 per hour.

"The high price of milk" – why do people use the word high? The price of milk is much lower than the price of beer. You do not get a quart of beer for 22 cents. We can't think of any good drinkable fluid which sells at 22 cents per quart, home delivered, except milk.

The fact of the matter, we suppose, is that milk is one of those emotional words. "Cheaper milk!" shout the politicians as they look for votes.

J. BROWN
Local 464, Milk Sales Drivers and Dairy Employees Union,
Vancouver, April 13, 1955

Another crusade – Cheaper Drugs, or better still, a comprehensive national health service. The price of drugs is a great shock to one coming from a country like England, where the National Health Service is now well established and is proving a great benefit to the majority of people.

Who benefits from the high cost of drugs and medical treatment in this country? The patient? Very doubtful.

Surely the patient is the one who must be considered first.

CRUSADER,
Sardis, July 7, 1955

— The Province

Empire Stadium, 1964

The Beatles hit town in August to play to 16,000 hysterical fans. A local scribe reports that the Fab Four uses 'every cheap theatrical trick … over-amplified guitars, wild drumming, hysterical singing and erotic posturing.' During the 20-minute scream-fest, 185 teens and pre-teens are injured and treated for hysteria, cuts and bruises.

YEAH YEAH YEAH

BY DAMIAN INWOOD

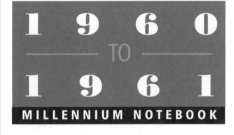
The era of the Kennedy assassinations, men on the moon and Woodstock marks the start of a media-fuelled age. Television brings the horror of the Vietnam War into our living rooms and we watch with macabre fascination as world events unfold before our eyes.

Whether it's John F. Kennedy being shot, napalm bombing in Southeast Asia, Beatlemania or the civil rights marches of Dr. Martin Luther King, we see it.

In B.C., growth continues as Vancouver starts to change from a town driven by lumber exports to a West Coast metropolis.

High-rises are sprouting and in the West End, run-down homes are making way for apartment blocks.

Typhoon Frieda comes barrelling out of the Pacific in the fall of 1962, toppling trees and causing $10 million damage with gusts of up to 114 km/h.

In 1963, the B.C. Lions make it to the Grey Cup final but lose out 21-10 to the Hamilton Tiger-Cats. The following year the Lions win their first Grey Cup by mauling the T-Cats 34-24.

Predictably, the Beatles concert that opens the 1964 PNE fair turns into a melee of screaming, fainting youth.

A major 1965 event is the opening of the Arthur Erikson-designed Simon Fraser University, which quickly gains a reputation as a hotbed of left-wing doctrine.

In 1966, home-grown hero Elaine Tanner, West Vancouver's "Mighty Mouse," wins four gold and three silver medals at the British Empire Games in Jamaica.

As the anti-Vietnam War movement grows in the U.S., Canada becomes a refuge for draft dodgers and deserters.

The West Coast becomes the magnet for kids who want to turn on, tune in and drop out in the 1967 Summer of Love.

The "Swinging Sixties" follow, when tie-dye, bell-bottoms and Afro hairstyles became de rigueur and Haight-Ashbury sets the pace in San Francisco.

It all comes to a head when hundreds of thousands descend on a New York State farm in 1969 for Woodstock.

That same year, millions of residents in the global village are transfixed by events on the moon.

U.S. astronaut Neil Armstrong steps on to the lunar landscape on July 20, 1969, and utters a phrase that becomes part of our culture: "That's one small step for man, one giant leap for mankind."

> **Predictably, the Beatles concert that opens the 1964 PNE fair turns into a melee of screaming, fainting youth**

1960

Feb. 1: Four black college students "sit-in" after they're refused service at the "whites only" Woolworths counter in Greensboro, N.C., inspiring similar actions across the South.

March 21: South African police open fire on black demonstrators in the Johannesburg suburb of Sharpeville, killing 56 demonstrators and wounding 162, including 16 who die later.

Mar. 29: A jury sentences Richard Hickock and Perry Smith to death for the killings of Herbert Clutter, wife Bonnie, daughter Nancy and son Kenyon. The

VIETNAM: CANADA PROFITS

Canadian companies sell the U.S. $2.5 billion in munitions, including ammunition, explosives and napalm for U.S. use in the Vietnam War.

They provide another $10 billion in food, beverages, berets and boots, plus nickel, copper, lead, brass and oil, for shell casings, wiring, plate armour and military transport.

Unemployment in Canada falls to a record low of 3.9 per cent.

Meanwhile, U.S. companies invest $3 billion in Canada.

The herbicide Agent Orange is tested at CFB Gagetown in New Brunswick and U.S. bombers practise carpet bombing runs over Canadian prairie bases.

About 10,000 Canadians fight in the U.S. armed forces during the war. About 20,000 U.S. draft dodgers and 12,000 army deserters cross the border into Canada.

The last day of Camelot

"The world has been plunged into a state of grief and shock by the assassination of John. F. Kennedy," says *The Province's* front page story. In Dallas, Tex., reporter Ed Johnson writes: "We could see spectators lining the route fall to the ground as the shots rang out. A woman roughly knocked her two children to the ground. A man, apparently her husband, lay beside them, pounding his fist into the earth." On Nov. 22, 1963, U.S. President John F. Kennedy is pronounced dead and shocked Vancouver residents gather to talk about it. "This was the feeling of the city: A friend was lost," adds *The Province,* as TV stations cancel commercials as a mark of respect. In Dallas, police arrest Lee Harvey Oswald, a 24-year-old school book-depository worker. He is fatally shot two days later in a Dallas jail by nightclub owner Jack Ruby as millions watch on TV.

— Knight-Ridder

President and Jacqueline Kennedy arrive in Dallas on Nov. 22, 1963.

family died from shotgun blasts in their home in Holcomb, Kan., on Nov. 15, 1959. The murders and trial will become the subject of Truman Capote's book In *Cold Blood.*

May 1: A Soviet missile brings down a CIA U-2 spy plane piloted by Francis Gary Powers. In a trial broadcast worldwide, the Soviets convict Powers of espionage. He is sentenced to 10 years' "deprivation of freedom" but is exchanged for Soviet spy Rudolph Abel in 1962.

May 11: Israeli secret agents seize Ricardo Clement in Argentina, spirit him to Israel and identify him as Nazi Adolf Eichmann, who oversaw the Holocaust. Eichmann is hanged May 31, 1962, saying: "I was just following orders."

July 1: Canadian Treaty Indians receive the right to vote.

Aug. 4: The Canadian Bill of Rights is approved by the House of Commons and receives royal assent on Aug. 10.

Dec. 5: Anette Toft, 16, arrives from Denmark to become Canada's two millionth

immigrant since the end of the Second World War.

1961

Jan. 17: The Columbia River Treaty is signed between Canada and the U.S. Three flood-control dams will be built in B. C. and power stations will be built in Washington State. Thirteen communities will be relocated, 2,300 people displaced and 60,000 hectares flooded.

Gagarin

April 12: Soviet Cosmonaut Yuri Gagarin, 27, is the first human launched into Earth orbit.

Aug. 3: The New Democratic Party is created by merging the Co-operative Commonwealth Federation (CCF) and the Canadian Labour Congress, with Tommy Douglas as leader.

Aug. 13: Soldiers string barbed wire across the border between communist East Berlin and the western sector. Eventually, it is replaced by concrete walls and electrified fences and is called the Berlin Wall.

BOOKS

POISONING THE LAND

Environmental prophet and marine biologist Rachel Carson asks readers, in her bestseller *Silent Spring,* to imagine a place where no birds sing, hens' eggs never hatch and apple trees bear no fruit.

The book alerts millions to the dangers of poisons such as DDT that are now widely used.

MEDICINE

WOMEN GET THE PILL

A sexual revolution is about to erupt in this new, tumultuous decade, and science makes it possible. The arrival of the world's first effective oral contraceptive gives women mastery over "that ol' devil, the female reproductive system," says Katherine McCormick, an heiress who helped support research on it.

CELEBRITIES

A BRITISH INVASION

Four Britons called the Beatles plunder the hearts of gaggles of screeching young North American females in 1964. The thick-thatched foursome—Paul McCartney, Ringo Starr, John Lennon and George Harrison — become instant celebrities and sell 2.5 million albums in less than a month. Their tour includes a concert at Empire Stadium in Vancouver.

DEATH OF A GODDESS

On Aug. 5, 1962, at age 36, the cinema goddess born as Norma Jean Baker and known to the world as Marilyn Monroe is found dead at her Los Angeles home, a bottle of sleeping pills at her side.

PASSAGES

Sir Winston Spencer Churchill, Britain's indomitable Second World War leader and perhaps the greatest Englishman of the 20th century, dies Jan. 24, 1965, in London after a stroke at age 90. Leaders from 110 nations attend the funeral at St. Paul's Cathedral.

ENTERTAINMENT

THE WOODSTOCK SPIRIT

In a field near Bethel, N.Y., a new "nation" is conceived during the long weekend of Aug. 15-18, 1969. It is dedicated to the proposition that all young people are entitled to free music, free food and—for those who want them—drugs.

The Woodstock Music and Art Fair—or simply Woodstock—is a disastrously underplanned concert event that becomes a touchstone for the burgeoning counterculture as well as the largest event of its kind.

Woodstock becomes a free "happening" when organizers and New York state police underestimate the turnout: 200,000 to 300,000 show up, trampling fences and overwhelming attempts to control access to the site. Traffic is so bad that helicopters are pressed into service to deliver food, water, medicine and even the performers. There is both a conventional first-aid tent and a Freak-Out Tent for drug overdoses. The fact that

only three deaths are reported is considered remarkable. Even a rainstorm does not dampen the spirit.

PRODUCTS

NEW IN 1969:
- Boeing 747 jumbo jet; first commercial flight Dec. 2 from Seattle to New York.
- *Penthouse* magazine.
- Automatic teller machines, at Chemical Bank, New York.

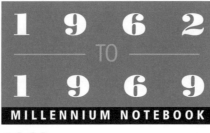

1962 TO 1969
MILLENNIUM NOTEBOOK

1962
Feb. 20: John Glenn Jr. rides the Mercury capsule *Friendship* 7 into earth orbit.
March 2: Philadelphia Warriors player Wilt Chamberlain becomes the first basketball player to score 100 points in a game.
March 21: The drug thalidomide is withdrawn from the market for a year as there is evidence that it may cause birth defects. By the end of July, Saskatchewan, Alberta and Ontario promise assistance to affected parents.
April 16: Walter Cronkite makes his debut as anchor on the CBS Evening News.
Oct. 22: The Cuban missile crisis begins when U.S. President John F. Kennedy announces a blockade of Cuba because of Soviet missiles on the island. Canada's air defences are put on high alert from Oct. 24 and tension continues until Oct. 28, when Soviet President Nikita Khrushchev agrees to remove the missiles.
Dec. 11: The last hanging in Canada sees Ronald Turpin and Arthur Lucas executed in Toronto for murder.

1963
April 20: The radical separatist group Front de Liberation du Quebec (FLQ) plants a bomb at a Montreal army recruiting centre. The blast kills Wilfred O'Neil.
Aug. 28: Dr. Martin Luther King Jr. gives his "I have a dream" speech before the Lincoln Memorial, where 300,000 people have gathered for the March on Washington. The next year he wins the Nobel Peace Prize.

1964
Feb. 25: Cassius Clay, an 8-1 underdog to heavyweight champion Sonny Liston, "floats like a butterfly, stings like a bee" to hammer Liston in a bout in Miami Beach. Later, Clay becomes a Muslim and changes his name to Muhammad Ali.
March 14: Jack Ruby is sentenced to death for killing Lee Harvey Oswald, alleged assassin of President Kennedy.
March 28: A tidal wave sweeps up Alberni

Inlet and strikes Port Alberni, causing millions of dollars in damage.
Dec. 15: The Maple Leaf flag becomes Canada's official flag. It will be flown for the first time at Parliament Hill on Feb. 15, 1965.

1965
Jan. 1: Trans-Canada Airlines changes its name to Air Canada.
April 15: 15,000 young people picket the White House, demanding U.S. troops get out of Vietnam.
July 8: A bomb explodes on a Canadian Pacific flight causing the plane to crash into Gustafsen Lake, killing all 52 on board.
Aug. 11: A white policeman in Watts, Los Angeles, stops a black man suspected of drunk driving, sparking five days of violence, leaving 34 dead, hundreds injured, 200 businesses destroyed and property damage of $200 million US.
Sept. 15: Bill Cosby becomes the first African-American to star in a weekly TV drama when *I Spy* makes its debut on NBC.
Nov. 9: A failure at an Ontario Hydro power station causes a 13-hour blackout, affecting New York, New England, parts of New Jersey, Pennsylvania, Ontario and Quebec. It is credited with a baby boom nine months later.

1966
April 11: Jack Nicklaus is the first golfer to win consecutive Masters tournaments.
July 19: Entertainer Frank Sinatra, 50, marries actress Mia Farrow, 21, in Las Vegas.
Aug. 1: A student at the University of Texas's Austin campus shoots students, teachers and visitors from a tower. Charles Whitman is shot by police. Earlier that day, he had killed his wife and mother. The toll is 16 dead, including Whitman, and 31 wounded.
Aug. 29: The Beatles play their last live concert at Candlestick Park, San Francisco.
Oct 1: CBC TV begins broadcasting in colour.

1967
April 12: "O Canada" becomes the national anthem.
May 1: Elvis Presley and Priscilla Beaulieu marry.
July 1: Canada celebrates its centennial.
July 24: French President Charles de

A man on the moon

Edwin (Buzz) Aldrin with a U.S. flag beside the lunar module.

— NASA

Throughout the world on a wondrous July Sunday, people gather around radios and TV screens, waiting—with a sense of awe—for what is arguably the most significant event of the 20th century: The human species is setting foot on a world beyond its own.

At 1:17:42 p.m. Pacific time, July 20, 1969, the four spindly legs of the lunar module Eagle touch down on the moon's powdery surface. The words sound tinny across the vastness of space, but they are electrifying. "Houston, Tranquility Base here," says Apollo 11 commander Neil Armstrong. "The Eagle has landed."

At ball games and picnics, on street corners and living rooms, wherever there might be a transistor radio or a TV, people whoop and cheer—or weep—filled with pride and wonder. At 7:56:20 p.m, Armstrong puts the first human footprint on the moon. "That's one small step for man, one giant leap for mankind," he says, inadvertently dropping the "a" before "man."

An estimated 528 million people, the largest TV audience ever, watch as a ghostly white figure makes the first steps in a barren, alien landscape. He is followed down the lunar module's ladder by Air Force Col. Edwin E. "Buzz" Aldrin Jr. They plant a flag, collect samples, snap photos and gambol about in the moon's light gravity.

After 21½ hours on the Sea of Tranquility, the lunar module's top section blasts off and rejoins the command ship with Air Force Lt. Col. Michael Collins aboard.

'Vive le Quebec libre': Charles de Gaulle in Montreal in 1967.

— Canadian Press

Gaulle ends a speech on the balcony of Montreal City Hall with the phrase "Vive le Quebec libre." Prime Minister Lester Pearson sends de Gaulle home, stating that his words were "unacceptable to the Canadian people and its government."

Nov. 9: With $7,000 US borrowed from an uncle, Jann Wenner, 21, launches Rolling Stone. The debut cover has a portrait of John Lennon wearing a Second World War-vintage British helmet.

Dec. 3: South African heart surgeon Christiaan Barnard takes the heart from brain-dead accident victim Denise Ann Darvall and puts it into the chest of Louis Washkansky in the world's first successful human heart transplant.

June 5: The Six Day War breaks out between Israel and Arab neighbours. Israel breaks the back of Arab air power and captures the West Bank, Golan Heights, Gaza Strip, Sinai Peninsula and the Old City of Jerusalem. A June 10 ceasefire ends the war.

1968

March 16: At a South Vietnamese hamlet, My Lai, members of Charlie Company, 11th Brigade, America 1 Division massacre between 109 and 567 civilians, including babies.

April 6: Pierre Trudeau is made leader of the Liberal party. On June 25 he leads the Liberals to an election victory and Trudeaumania begins.

June 24: The St-Jean-Baptiste Day riots occur in Montreal; 290 are arrested and 130 injured.

Aug. 27: At the Chicago Democratic convention, about 3,000 anti-war demonstrators clash with police and Illinois National Guardsmen. Police use clubs and tear gas while protesters hurl rocks and break car windows.

Oct. 13: The release of Apple Records' Two Virgins, with John Lennon and wife Yoko Ono nude on the cover, causes a furore.

1969

March 10: James Earl Ray pleads guilty to the murder of Dr. Martin Luther King Jr. and is sentenced to 99 years in prison.

April 27: Sirhan Bishara Sirhan is convicted in Los Angeles of the 1968 murder of Sen. Robert Kennedy. Later, he is sentenced to die in the gas chamber.

July 19: A car driven by Sen. Edward Kennedy plunges off a bridge as he and aide Mary Jo Kopechne, 28, are leaving a cookout at Chappaquiddick Island off Massachusetts. Kennedy pleads guilty to leaving the scene of the accident in which Kopechne died and is given a two-month suspended sentence but the incident kills his presidential plans.

Dec. 8: Charles Manson, 35, and five followers are indicted in the murders of seven people. Four months earlier, police had gone to a mansion in Benedict Canyon, Calif., and found the bodies of five people, including actress Sharon Tate, followed by the discovery of two more bodies the next day.

— The Province

STANLEY PARK, 1968 On Easter Day, April 14, the hippies arrive in Stanley Park for the Super-Human Be-In. It's the first Be-In held in Stanley Park and 1,500 vibed-out people arrive to burn incense and joss sticks, listen to rock music and invent the twirly dance. The decade was marked elsewhere by protests against the war in Vietnam, peace rallies, university sit-ins and marches.

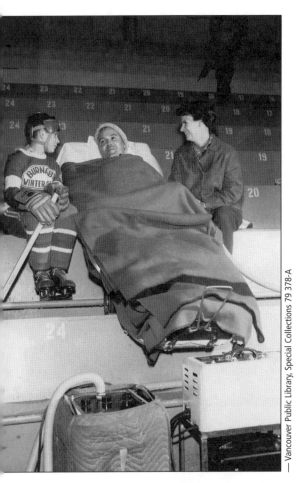

— Vancouver Public Library, Special Collections 79 378-A

THE FORUM, VANCOUVER, 1961 In this touching photo, polio victim Harry Watts prepares to watch his son play hockey for the Burnaby Winter Club. Watts is taken to the arena via station wagon, complete with portable iron lung equipment, to see his son's first hockey game.

Polio cruelly paralyzed and killed thousands before a vaccine was developed in the early 1950s. Between 1927 and 1962 there were nearly 15,000 registered cases in B.C. Most of the survivors still living in B.C. today fell ill in the early 1950s and spent time in the iron lungs at Vancouver's George Pearson Centre. Pearson today continues to care for more seriously affected polio patients.

Watts died during the 1970s.

VANCOUVER, 1970 Street photographer Foncie Pulice, a fixture in Vancouver for 45 years, plies his trade on Granville Street. Pulice worked the streets from 1934 to 1979, eventually running three businesses taking as many as 8,000 black-and-white photos a day. In time, these pictures become precious mementoes for Vancouver residents or visitors walking Theatre Row on the "Great White Way," as Granville is known. Foncie retires in 1979 and moves to Kelowna, where he lives today, aged 85.

— Vancouver Sun

1960

A government-owned ferry service begins on the Tsawwassen-Victoria route. Says a senior politician to *The Province*, "We wish to heck we weren't in the ferry business."

The new Second Narrows Bridge, still in use today, opens Aug. 25. A total of 18 ironworkers died when the bridge collapsed during construction in 1958.

In October, Nanaimo's Chinese shantytown is destroyed in that city's biggest fire. The blaze leaves 250 refugees homeless.

Brentwood Mall, the largest in B.C, opens in Burnaby.

1961

The Trail Smoke Eaters win the world amateur hockey championships in March, beating Russia 5-1 in Geneva. It is the second world championship for Trail, which also won in 1939.

In October, the RCMP raid libraries and bookstores in search of a banned book: Henry Miller's *Tropic of Cancer.*

1962

Although construction is still in progress, the Trans-Canada Highway is declared complete and opened Sept. 3 with a $40 million link from Revelstoke to Golden.

In August, the first Abbotsford air show attracts 14,000 viewers.

Typhoon Frieda wreaks havoc on the Lower Mainland, causing seven deaths. Stanley Park loses 20 per cent of its evergreens. They're replaced by maples and alders, changing the park forever.

At the Empire Games, gold medals go to Vancouver swimmer Mary Stewart and Prince George boxer George Harold Mann.

1963

April 2 marks the end of tolls on Lions Gate Bridge.

1964

A tsunami hits Port Alberni, causing mass flooding and property damage.

At the Tokyo Olympics, U.B.C. rowers George Hungerford and Roger Jackson win gold and Richmond's Harry Jerome gets a bronze for the 100-metre dash. Doug Rogers gets a silver medal in judo.

In November, the B.C. Lions win their first Grey Cup.

40 KILOMETRES WEST OF 100-MILE HOUSE, 1965

An explosion aboard a routine flight from Vancouver to Prince George on July 8 causes a crash that kills all 52 people aboard. RCMP investigators spend 10 months probing backgrounds of all 52 victims, questioning hundreds of people and exploring dozens of theories from suicide for insurance to syndicate murder. All they establish is that the explosion of an object foreign to the DC-6B airliner in the port bathroom tore the tail from the plane and caused it to spiral 5,000 metres into the woods. The mystery of CPA Flight 21 remains unsolved.

— The Province

VANCOUVER COURTHOUSE, 1962

Doukhobors—isolationists who believe there should be no government intervention in their lives—talk to friends outside the courthouse. During the 1950s and '60s, the Doukhobors (their radical members are known as the Sons of Freedom) cause a furore after holding nude protests and burning buildings, many of them their own. This scene is the result of protests over compulsory education in British Columbia. Members of the religious sect (they believe in pacifism and simple, communal living) are shipped off to Agassiz's Mountain Institute in the early '60s, convicted of arson and terrorism.

— Vancouver Public Library, Special Collections 2871

— The Province

FALSE CREEK, 1960 A $2-million, wind-whipped fire tears through the spruce division of B.C. Forest Products in July, spreading over an area of three city blocks. It wipes out sheds, kilns and millions of board-feet of lumber. It is the first five-alarm fire in the city's history and Fire Chief Hugh Bird describes it as the worst blaze he's seen in his 33 years on the job. 250 men are put to work bringing it under control and 10,000 sightseers turn out to witness the effort.

1965

In January, a wall of rock, timber and snow roars down a mountain, engulfing the Hope-Princeton Highway and killing four motorists. It takes 21 days to reopen the highway.

In February, an avalanche kills 26 miners at the Granduc Mine installation in a remote section of northern B.C.

Simon Fraser University opens Sept. 9 on Burnaby Mountain.

Grace MacInnis becomes B.C.'s first female MP.

1966

Grouse Mountain opens a gondola that carries up to 50 passengers at a time, and Whistler's first ski lift opens.

1967

Canada's centennial celebrations begin Jan. 9 in Victoria, where the Centennial Train begins a cross-Canada tour.

On June 1, Canada's first McDonald's restaurant opens in Richmond. Hamburgers cost 18 cents each.

On Canada's 100th birthday, Chief Dan George of the Burrard Indian Reserve silences a crowd of 32,000 with his "Lament for Confederation" at Empire Stadium. George's mournful speech begins with, "Today, when you celebrate your hundred years, oh Canada, I am sad for all the Indian people throughout the land."

Greenpeace is founded in the Dunbar area under the name "Don't Make a Wave Committee."

1968

Skier Nancy Greene, from Rossland, wins a gold and a silver at the Grenoble Olympics and returns home to a hero's welcome.

1969

Elaine "Mighty Mouse" Tanner, an 18-year old from Vancouver, retires from swimming with three Olympic medals and five world records.

–Melissa Radler

RICHMOND, 1968 Two people die and 18 are hurt when a Canadian Pacific Airlines Boeing 707 bounces off a foggy runway at Vancouver International Airport on Feb. 7, 1968. The plane, arriving from Hawaii, cuts a 1.5-km path of destruction across the airport on its way to crashing into an empty building. One crew member and one transport department ground worker die in the crash. At one point the 90-tonne aircraft is heading for the busy passenger terminal before slewing to the right and into the building.

Gordon Sedawie — The Province

QUEENS PARK, NEW WESTMINSTER, 1960 Cold War paranoia is alive and well in B.C. as Chilliwack Army Corp. Engineers stage a mock atomic explosion and rescue demonstration, replete with nuke-proof tin helmets and khaki radiation suits (sleeves rolled up). Elsewhere, radiation monitoring officers are explaining the operation of Geiger counters at schools (students are instructed to duck under their desks if the bombs are dropped) and families are studying *Your Basement Fallout Shelter: Blueprint For Survival No. 1.*

— Vancouver Public Library, Special Collections 79792-B

Bridge game

Correspondence, articles and announcements about a new crossing for First Narrows are continually appearing, but nowhere have I seen any mention of a very important fact: the time when the existing Lions Gate Bridge will become unfit for further use.

When this happens it will be a first-class opportunity to close the park to through traffic once and for all. It could then remain in peace and quiet, to Vancouver's advantage.

If another bridge is built near the present one it is obvious that this opportunity will be lost possibly for all time, and the park will be chopped up even more by further roads to the new bridge.

Looking ahead to such a day, it is quite obvious that a bridge from Brockton Point locality is much more logical and it is to be hoped that when such a bridge is built it will be designed for adequate capacity, perhaps allowing for additional decks to be added later.

JOHN SMITH
Vancouver, Nov. 5, 1965

Would a good birching stop you criminals?

Now, when the criminals have declared open season on law and order, would it not be a good thing to revive the lash or the strap?

The holdup men and those convicted of murder, rape and assault on policemen and citizens should be given a taste of it.

The politicians in Ottawa have taken on themselves to abolish the death penalty for murder. The worst they can get now is a vacation in New Westminster, where they are fed and have a warm place to sleep.

For the young vandals and purse-snatchers maybe a good birching, so they can't sit down for a day or two, would be a good deterrent.

FED UP
Vancouver, Feb. 3, 1965

When Canada's new flag was being chosen, Alberta bus driver John Heysel offered a design featuring a beaver, a tree and maple leaves.

— The Province

Death of an era

Pearson's house flag will be officially broken out today. I would suggest that all British Columbians buy a Red Ensign and fly it at half mast and upside down to indicate the death of an era and a country in distress.

UPAN ATEM
West Vancouver,
Feb. 15, 1965

The Beatles

Further to the awarding of the MBE to the Beatles, an article in the *Saturday Evening Post* quotes their press officer, Derrick Taylor, as saying: "Here are these four boys from Liverpool. They are rude, they're profane, they're vulgar and they've taken over the world. It's as if they've founded a new religion. They're completely anti-Christ. I mean, I'm anti-Christ as well, but they're so anti-Christ they shock me, which isn't an easy thing."

Maybe we're all wrong about what medal they were given. Maybe it was the MBE—the Medal of Barbaric Egotism!

J.P.T.
June 18, 1965

Gasoline playground

Whither do we drift?

The equestrian has vanished and the pedestrian is on his last legs. We are engulfed now by a multitude of cars and noxious fumes are inescapable.

WILLIAM CROFTON
Vancouver, March 6, 1965

Raise bus fares

About 25 years ago the average man earned about 60 cents an hour, and at that time I think the bus fares were seven cents. Today they are 20 cents.

Do you think 20 cents is enough to pay when the average wage is $3 an hour or more?

Remember that a lot of people do not use the bus. Why should they have to stand the loss on the buses? I think they should send their children out with placards when the different trades ask for an increase in wages.

SUBSCRIBER
Vancouver, Jan. 9, 1965

Smart girls

I see where a learned professor told the Learned Societies at UBC that a girl should always marry up and a man down for a successful marriage.

This makes it pretty tough for a really intelligent girl to get a husband.

FATHER OF THREE
SMART GIRLS
West Vancouver, June 18, 1965

Drunk driving

Coroner Glen McDonald is so right about drunken driving and the law.

It all boils down to a deterrent in the form of a chemical test. We are getting closer to the moment of truth. The greatest problem may be the bar itself, which has a very

Highway deaths

Perhaps the shocking figure of 62 highway deaths in July will make drivers realize that once they are behind the wheel they are not the monarchs they think they are.

Ray Hadfield, superintendent of the motor vehicle branch, has put the blame on "selfish motorists with a flagrant disregard for the law and the rights of others."

As a truck driver, I see examples of this "flagrant disregard for the law" every day. I see drunken drivers, persons driving at excessive speeds and all too many "road hogs." I also see the results of their foolishness.

Perhaps one of these days motorists will wake up to the fact that they too can become a statistic.

HIBALLER
Vancouver, Aug. 7, 1965

real responsibility in these matters to protect the personal freedom of individuals, and may become a little confused as to whose personal freedom it is most important to protect.

This particular problem is getting close to a wartime footing, where we must forgo certain liberties for the good of the general community.

ROBERT E. MALKIN
Vancouver, March 6, 1965

Here's a *real* boon for the human race

Scientists keep on with marvels of spaceships and mechanical brains and electronic gadgets, and it's all very wonderful. Colour television, rockets to Mars, dishwashing thingamajigs.

But I don't want to go to Mars. I don't like watching TV and a wife's pretty lazy if she can't wash a few dishes. What I want invented is a lawn that would stay nice and green—but that wouldn't grow.

PROGRESSIVE
Vancouver, Aug. 16, 1965

Uninterested

The fact that the Pearson government has not passed legislation to make (drug) trafficking punishable by life imprisonment proves how completely uninterested it is in people and expense, since drug addiction is one of Canada's most costly problems.

A REALIST
Vancouver, Nov. 5, 1965

On women

With all due respect to Ethel Slater, her letter (Aug. 4) is an attempt to justify the women of today.

I have lived long enough to see what a change freedom to vote has made in the women of our land. I am glad I am old and can remember the dear aunts, uncles and other folk of past days when women were ladies.

E. MACLEAN
Vancouver, Aug. 7, 1965

Bill Cunningham — The Province

Vancouver, 1971

The Province breaks the news of Prime Minister Pierre Elliott Trudeau's wedding to Vancouver's Margaret Sinclair with this front-page picture on March 4, 1971. Trudeau and the 22-year-old Sinclair are secretly wed in a Lynn Valley Catholic church after dating for three years. They had met while on holiday in Tahiti in 1968. The priest and wedding photographer are told Sinclair will be marrying a "Pierre Mercier."

P.M. GETS HITCHED

By Damian Inwood

fter the tumult of the '60s, life in the '70s seems duller, with the beat of a disco generation setting the tone.

A benchmark is the Vancouver Canucks joining the NHL in 1970. They lose their opening game to the Los Angeles Kings 3-1. A sign of things to come?

Canada is rocked by the FLQ kidnappings of Pierre Laporte and James Cross, leading to the introduction of the War Measures Act.

But our spirits are briefly lifted in 1972 by Team Canada's last-gasp defeat of the Soviet hockey team and Paul Henderson's goal.

In B.C., Dave Barrett's NDP government defeats W.A.C. Bennett's Socreds and the Insurance Corp. of B.C.'s Autoplan is born.

Barrett is kicked out by voters in 1975 after a series of labour confrontations, capped off by a B.C. Ferries dispute. Taking over is W.A.C.'s son, Bill Bennett.

In a decade where the phrases "wage and price controls" and "sovereignty association" will become a familiar part of our lexicon, the beaver becomes the official symbol of Canada in 1975.

An era ends when Eaton's catalogue sales end in 1976, but Canada wins its first Oscar for a feature film with *The Man Who Skied Down Everest.* Mother Teresa visits Vancouver as part of Habitat, a United Nations conference on human settlements.

For the first time since 1939, the Canadian dollar sinks below 90 cents U.S. in 1977. The Bank of Canada moves to prop it up.

The Vietnam War ends but the U.S. also seems to be in the '70s doldrums.

Low points include Watergate and the resignation of Richard Nixon, the Niagara Falls Love Canal pollution scandal, and New York mass murderer David Berkowitz—the Son of Sam.

In Canada it's the decade of "Joe Who?" A young Albertan named Joe Clark comes from obscurity to win the Progressive Conservative leadership. He goes on to defeat Pierre Trudeau's Liberals and forms a minority government in 1979.

We all have five BCRIC ("Brick") energy resource shares, courtesy of the Socreds, who almost lose a bitter 1979 election campaign, winning by just four seats over Barrett's NDPers.

The decade ends with the angry snarls of punk, taking over from disco and arena rock.

> Canada is rocked by the FLQ kidnappings of Pierre Laporte and James Cross, leading to the introduction of the War Measures Act

1970

April 13: En route to the moon, *Apollo 13* crew members hear an explosion in the service module, which houses the ship's main engine and most of its life-giving power systems. The lunar module becomes the crew's lifeboat for most of the journey home. *Apollo 13* splashes down safely in the Pacific on April 17.

May 22: The Vancouver Canucks join the NHL.

June 26: The Canada Elections Act lowers the age of voting to 18 from 21.

July 5: An Air Canada DC-8 loses an engine during landing at Toronto International Airport. When the pilot attempts to take off and land again, the second engine drops off. The plane crashes, killing all 109 people on board.

1971

Jan. 2: A soccer match in Glasgow ends in tragedy when a stadium barrier collapses and 66 people are trampled to death.

March 4: Prime Minister Pierre Trudeau, 51, marries Margaret Sinclair, 22, in North Vancouver.

March 29: U.S. Army 1st Lieut. William Calley is found guilty in a military court of the murders of 22 Vietnamese civilians in the My Lai massacre. He is the only soldier convicted, although a number of officers and enlisted personnel are tried.

Oct. 1: Disney World opens in Orlando, Fla., costing close to $600 million US.

1972

Jan. 5: U.S. President Nixon signs a bill for a $5.5-billion US, six-year program to develop a space shuttle that will lift off as a rocket and return as an airplane.

Jan. 30: On "Bloody Sunday," British troops kill 13 men in Londonderry, Northern Ireland, during a Roman Catholic civil rights rally. On March 24, Britain dissolves Northern Ireland's provincial government and orders direct rule from London.

May 1: The Supreme Court of Canada rules that breathalyser tests do not breach the Bill of Rights.

Trudeau: 'Just watch me'

Prime Minister Pierre Trudeau knocks on the roof of his bullet-proof car in Ottawa on Oct. 13, 1970, after switching from his regular car to an armoured Cadillac in the wake of FLQ terrorist activity.

— Canadian Press

The October Crisis hits Canada when the Front de Liberation du Quebec kidnaps British envoy James Cross in Montreal on Oct. 5, 1970.

The kidnappers demand the release of detained FLQ members and the broadcast of a manifesto.

Five days later, Quebec labour minister Pierre Laporte is kidnapped and his body is found Oct. 17 in the trunk of a car.

Asked how far he will go to fight the FLQ, Prime Minister Pierre Trudeau replies: "Just watch me."

He implements the War Measures Act on Oct. 16, suspending civil liberties and sending the armed forces into Quebec. Police arrest 450 people without charge in a huge manhunt for the kidnappers.

In December, the FLQ frees Cross, and one group of kidnappers is flown to exile in Cuba.

Four weeks later a second group is arrested and later tried and convicted of kidnapping and murder.

May 15: Alabama Gov. George C. Wallace, an independent presidential candidate who champions racial segregation, is shot and critically wounded after a campaign speech in Laurel, Md. The attack leaves him paralyzed from the waist down. On Aug. 4, Arthur Herman Bremer, 21, is convicted and given 63 years in prison.

Sept. 5: Palestinian guerrillas kill two Israeli athletes at the Olympic Village. Nine hostages, five captors and a policeman die in gunfire at an airfield in Munich, West Germany. The XX Olympiad is suspended for two days.

1973

Jan. 22: The U.S. Supreme Court rules that personal privacy rights are "broad enough to encompass a woman's decision whether or not to terminate her pregnancy." The Roe vs. Wade decision invalidates abortion statutes in 46 U.S. states.

Jan. 27: A Vietnam peace agreement is signed in Paris. The United States agrees to withdraw its 23,700-member force within 60 days. North Vietnam agrees to free more than 500 U.S. POWs.

May 8: Members of the American Indian Movement end a 71-day occupation at a reservation in South Dakota, where gunfire killed two FBI agents and wounded 12 others. Nearly 1,200 are arrested. The showdown is at Wounded Knee, site of a historic 1890 battle that killed 153 Sioux.

June 9: Secretariat, touted as "the greatest horse that ever lived," becomes the ninth horse to win racing's Triple Crown.

SPORTS

HENDERSON SCORES!

Canadians never forget where they were on Sept. 28, 1972, when a last-minute goal by Paul Henderson (right) won the Summit Series over the U.S.S.R.

The voice of TV commentator Foster Hewitt sums up a moment etched in sports history: "Here's a shot. Henderson makes a wild stab for it and falls. Here's another shot. Right in front. They score! Henderson scores for Canada!"

Team Canada defeats the Soviets 6-5 in the last 34 seconds of the final game in Moscow.

The series isn't always pretty.

As Canada loses the fourth game in Vancouver 4-3, the crowd boos the team off the ice.

Captain Phil Esposito is outraged and emotionally insists the team is giving "150 per cent."

ISSUES

BIRTH OF WOMEN'S LIB

Women's liberation is formalized in Canada in 1971 with the founding of the National Action Committee on the Status of Women. This umbrella group of 30 organizations later swells to 543 women's groups from all over Canada. It is formed a year after the 1970 release of a Royal Commission on the Status of Women. The Canadian women's magazine *Chatelaine* keeps pace with *Ms*, an upstart U.S. publication launched in 1972 by Gloria Steinem. Sex discrimination is banned in the 1978 Canadian Human Rights Act.

RELIGION

A NEW BIBLE

With trumpet fanfares in London's Westminster Abbey, leaders of the Protestant Churches of the British Isles are presented a new translation of the Bible. *The New English Bible* is the culmination of 24 years of work by British scholars. The aim is to make the Bible more relevant to contemporary readers, but some critics complain the new version lacks the majesty of the King James version of 1611.

WHAT'S IN VOGUE

In 1975, if you're not wearing a T-shirt touting some brand of beer, a sporting event or commercial enterprise, you're not cool. Leisure is in at the workplace: polyester suits for men;

sexy, tight-fitting fashions for women. Discotheques are the hot new clubs and more than 20 million mood rings (left), which change colour with body temperature, are sold in North America.

In 1976, a continent-wide craze for citizen's band radios has North Americans embracing such terms as "10-4" for affirmative, "good buddy" for an airwave acquaintance and "smokie" for a state trooper.

ENTERTAINMENT

NORTH AMERICA AND VCRS

Two competing Japanese companies introduce video-recording devices into the entertainment mix in 1976: Sony with Betamax, and JVC, or Japanese Victor Co., with VHS. The VCR dramatically broadens what people can watch on the tube. TV ad rates and movie attendance suffer, but the VCR is a boon to such emerging industries as video-rental stores and video pornography.

THE FORCE IS WITH YOU

R2D2

"A long time ago in a galaxy far, far away …" With those words in the opening titles, director George Lucas introduces filmgoers to the first instalment of his epic *Star Wars* series. The 1977 film, which grosses $232 million US in North America and millions more overseas, combines the elements of boys' adventure novels, Greek mythology, samurai epics, Westerns, pulp science fiction and matinee serials.

THE TUBE

TV GROWS UP

When CBS introduces *All in the Family* in 1971, critics consider it both a perfect reflection of the times and brilliantly ahead of its time. Middle-aged Archie Bunker is closed-minded and cigar-chomping, a working-class fella in Queens who isn't adapting to a changing world. *All in the Family* tops the ratings because it deals with all the issues of the times: feminism, peace, race, religion and marriage.

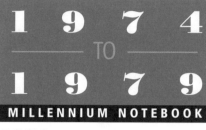

1974 TO 1979

MILLENNIUM NOTEBOOK

1974

Feb. 5: Patricia Hearst, daughter of publishing magnate Randolph Hearst, is kidnapped by the Symbionese Liberation Army. She is next seen April 15, during an armed bank robbery in San Francisco. It's unclear if she is a willing participant in the robbery.

May 5: NCR Corp. unveils the bar-code scanner at a Super Market Institute convention.

May 18: India detonates an atomic bomb and becomes the world's sixth nuclear power.

June 30: Mikhail Baryshnikov defects to the West while he is in Toronto as a guest artist with the Soviet Union's Bolshoi Ballet.

Aug. 5: The Watergate scandal climaxes when President Nixon admits to ordering a halt to the investigation of the burglary of the Watergate complex on June 17, 1972, at the Democratic Party's national headquarters. He says the order was for political as well as security reasons. The admission is contained in a statement accompanying the release of transcripts of three conversations taped on June 23, 1972.

Nixon resigns four days later, the first U.S. president to do so.

On Aug. 9, Vice-President Gerald Rudolph Ford assumes the presidency, becoming the first man in U.S. history to lead the nation without winning a national election.

Ford had been appointed to the vice-presidency after Spiro Agnew left office in disgrace.

Sept. 17: The RCMP accepts its first female recruits. Previously, women have only held civilian positions with the force.

Richard Nixon

1975

March 24: The beaver becomes the official symbol of Canada.

April 2: The CN Tower is completed in Toronto, making it the world's tallest free-standing structure at the time.

July 30: Former Teamsters Union leader Jimmy Hoffa disappears after being seen outside a restaurant in Bloomfield, Mich. He's rumoured to be buried in a cement highway overpass.

Sept. 5: In Sacramento, Calif., "Squeaky" Fromme, 26, a follower of jailed mass murderer Charles Manson, points a pistol at U.S. President Gerald Ford from close range. On Sept. 22, Ford escapes assassination when activist Sara Jane Moore, 45, fires a gun as he steps out of a San Francisco hotel.

Nov. 10: The 729-foot *Edmund Fitzgerald*, the largest ship on the Great Lakes, leaves Superior, Wis., with 26,000 tons of iron ore, bound for Detroit. In a terrible storm, 29 crewmen die as the vessel breaks in two and sinks. Canadian singer Gordon Lightfoot later records a hit song about the tragedy.

Nov. 18: Ontario introduces legislation making the wearing of seatbelts mandatory.

1976

Jan. 14: Eaton's discontinues its catalogue sales.

April 1: College dropouts Steve Jobs and Steve Wozniak form the Apple Computer Co. in Palo Alto, Calif. Working out of Jobs's garage, the two begin assembling Apple I computers, which sell for $666.66 US and have eight kilobytes of RAM.

A blindfolded American hostage is displayed outside the U.S. embassy in Teheran on Nov. 9, 1979.

Ambassador to the rescue

Taylor

When the U.S. embassy in Teheran is seized by Iranian revolutionaries on Nov, 4, 1979, a Canadian hero comes to the rescue.

Ken Taylor, Canada's ambassador in Iran, leads a daring plan to free six Americans who had managed to avoid capture when a mob of young Iranians broke into the U.S. compound and took 66 hostages.

Taylor, immigration officer John Sheardown and their wives hide the six U.S. embassy staff for two months. In what becomes known as "the Canadian Caper," the six Americans, with Taylor not far behind, leave Iran on Jan. 28, 1980, using Canadian passports.

The stylish, gregarious Taylor becomes an instant celebrity.

He receives the Order of Canada and the U.S. Congressional Gold Medal and becomes consul-general in New York from 1981 to 1984.

He is in constant demand on the TV talk show and lecture circuit.

The hostage-taking caps a year in which Iran is thrown into turmoil.

The Shah flees Jan. 16, 1979, after 37 years of U.S.-supported rule and Feb. 1, Ayatollah Ruhollah Khomeini takes power.

The Ayatollah declares an Islamic Republic, outlawing western freedoms and installing a strict regime of clerical rule.

The revolution creates an oil crisis and by summer, gasoline shortages spread throughout the world.

The crisis ends when the hostages are released Jan. 20, 1981, the day Ronald Reagan takes office as U.S. president.

June 16: Rioting erupts in the black South African township of Soweto over mandatory use of the Afrikaans language in schools. After three days, 60 are dead and 800 injured.

July 16: Capital punishment is abolished in Canada.

July 17: Queen Elizabeth II opens the Olympic summer games in Montreal. Romania's Nadia Comaneci scores perfect 10s in gymnastics and wins three gold medals. Canada is the first host country not to win gold.

Sept. 9: Mao Tse-tung, leader of China since 1949, dies of Parkinson's disease. An estimated one million flock into Tiananmen Square to mourn his death.

Nov. 17: The Parti Québécois, led by René Lévesque, wins a majority government in Quebec, ousting the Liberal party and Premier Robert Bourassa, who loses his own seat.

1977

March 27: A KLM Boeing 747 collides almost head-on with a taxiing Pan Am 747

on a fog-shrouded runway in the Canary Islands, killing 582 people in the worst aviation disaster in history.

Aug. 10: New York police arrest 24-year-old David Berkowitz for six murders. During the 13-month killing spree, Berkowitz calls himself Son of Sam in messages to police and newspapers. In 1978, he pleads guilty and gets 25 years to life for each killing.

Sept. 6: Road signs in Canada go metric for speed and distances, except in the provinces of Quebec and Nova Scotia.

Oct. 18: The Canadian House of Commons is first televised.

1978

Feb. 11: A Pacific Western Airlines plane crashes at Cranbrook, killing 43 people.

July 25: Louise Joy Brown is born in Oldham, England, the first baby conceived outside the womb by "in vitro fertilization."

Aug. 7: The Love Canal in Niagara Falls, N.Y., is unfit for human habitation. From 1947 to 1952, the Hooker Chemical Co. dumped toxic waste into an abandoned canal. In 1953, the company fills in the canal and sells it for $1 to Niagara Falls. The city builds a school and houses on the site.

Nov. 18: In Guyana, South America, 913 of cult leader Jim Jones's People's Temple followers commit mass "blue Kool Aid" suicide. Jones shoots himself.

1979

March 28: An accident occurs at Three Mile Island nuclear plant in Middletown, Pa. Within days, meltdown fears force 250,000 people to flee. A week later, officials stabilize the damaged reactor.

May 3: Margaret Thatcher, a grocer's daughter who became an Oxford-educated chemist and lawyer, becomes Britain's first female prime minister. She will remain in office 11 years.

May 22: The Conservative Party forms a minority government with Joe Clark as Canada's prime minister.

Aug. 27: The IRA kills Lord Louis Mountbatten, 79, great-grandson of Queen Victoria.

Dec. 10: Mother Teresa, a Roman Catholic nun who works with the poor in the slums of India, accepts the Nobel Peace Prize. "Personally, I am unworthy," the 69-year-old nun says. "I accept in the name of the poor."

Below: **NORTH VANCOUVER, 1973** Karen Magnussen, 20, comes home to a hero's welcome as world figure skating champion. The North Vancouver skater drives in a motorcade through the city and up to Centennial Theatre for a special reception. Premier Dave Barrett attends. Magnussen has already won silver at the 1972 Sapporo Olympics. She goes on to receive the Velma Springstead Trophy as Canada's outstanding woman athlete from 1971-73 and the Order of Canada.

Gordon Sedawie — The Province

VANCOUVER, 1979 An estimated 100,000 fans line downtown streets as the Vancouver Whitecaps return after winning the NASL Soccer Bowl. On a Sunday afternoon, a pickup truck carries team members and the trophy through the streets. The Whitecaps had defeated the Tampa Bay Rowdies 2-1 at Giants Stadium in New Jersey.

Right: **WEST VANCOUVER, 1973** About 180 tonnes of heavy bunker oil hits the shore and an emergency clean-up operation begins to save beaches from being fouled and to rescue wildlife. The oil slicks come from two ships, the *Erawan* and *Sun Diamond,* which collide off Point Grey. More than 2,000 metres of floating booms are stretched across the entrances to Fisherman's Cove and Eagle Harbour.

Ross Kenward — The Province

Colin Price — The Province

GRANVILLE MALL, 1974
Pedestrian precinct or commuter corridor? The what-should-we-do-with-it debate over Granville Mall begins in 1974 when the street is re-surfaced and narrowed to allow foot traffic only. In this picture, taken during Granville Mall's Aug. '74 opening, Vancouverites take a stroll down the city's central strip. Note how narrow the roadway is. Later, it is widened and buses and taxis are permitted back on the stretch. The debate over allowing cars to return continues today.

— The Province

1970

The Vancouver Canucks play their first NHL game. They lose to the Los Angeles Kings, 3-1.

Chief Dan George of North Vancouver's Burrard band is nominated for a best sup-porting actor Oscar for his performance in *Little Big Man.*

1971

Stanley Park's seawall is officially opened.

The Girl in Wet Suit sculpture is unveiled on a rock beside Stanley Park.

U.B.C. releases a report identifying the West End as the most densely populated square mile in Canada. Its population is 35,000.

B.C. now has 2,184,620 residents.

1972

The NDP, under leader Dave Barrett, defeats W.A.C. Bennett's Social Credit Party, which had been in power for 20 years.

Fran Cannon becomes the first woman to swim Georgia Strait.

1973

Jimmy Pattison buys the Philadelphia Blaz-ers of the WHA and moves the team to Vancouver. He names the team the Van-couver Blazers. It moves to Calgary in 1975.

1974

The Vancouver Whitecaps play their first game at Empire Stadium against the San Jose Earthquakes.

1975

The new B.C. Tel building, nicknamed "the boot" for its unusual design, starts to take shape at Kingsway and Bound-ary.

Sixty-one Vietnamese orphans arrive at the airport.

The False Creek seawall is completed.

Whistler receives the special designation of "resort municipality."

Prison employee Mary Steinhauser is killed during a riot at B.C. Penitentiary in New Westminster. She is one of 15 prison employees held hostage for 41 hours..
Steinhauser dies in a barrage of gunfire when guards storm the prisoners.

VANCOUVER, 1972
Police confiscate dozens of bottles of wine, beer and hard liquor, as well as knives, while searching fans on their way into a Rolling Stones concert at Pacific Coliseum. But the real trouble is with about 2,500 fans outside who fight a pitched battle, throwing rocks and firebombs, injuring about 30 police in the process. Inside, the show goes on and 17,000 fans get plenty of satisfaction.

Kenne Allen — The Province

Opposite: **VANCOUVER, 1973**
The last old-time English Bay cottage, built in 1906, is slated for demolition to make way for high-rise apartments. The homes on Beach Avenue are the last remaining links with the pre-concrete canyon era in the West End.

LONG BEACH, 1970 Hundreds of hippie squatters have turned Long Beach into a rag-tag shantytown. Driftwood labyrinths have sprung up and RCMP keep an eye on campers and people driving vehicles on the beach. Some of the kids are only 14 years old. Signs are stuck in the sand advertising marijuana and LSD for sale, says long-time beach resident Bill Billing at the time.

— The Province

Gordon Sadawie — The Province

COMING SOON.. ANOTHER CEMENT MONSTER

1975 continued:

British Columbians vote out Dave Barrett and the NDP and bring back the Socreds under Bill Bennett, son of former premier W.A.C. Bennett.

1975

Ladies can buy a pair of Florsheim shoes at Freedman's for just $21.99, while a new two-bedroom apartment on the 13th floor of Park Towers in Richmond rent for $365 a month.

And those wanting to get away from it all can take a seven-day Caribbean cruise for just $565, including airfare from Vancouver to Florida.

1976

Richmond's Arthur Laing Bridge opens.

U.B.C.'s Museum of Anthropology moves into its impressive new home, designed by Arthur Erickson.

As the Lower Mainland's suburban population grows, the city's population drops by about 300,000 since 1971. It is now 396,563.

1977

Vancouver Centre, at 651 feet above sea level, becomes the city's tallest structure.

1978

The Pacific Coast League of baseball gets a new team with the formation of the Vancouver Canadians.

The Gastown Steam Clock begins running on steam for the first time. It had been running on electricity since its installation a year earlier.

1979

Granville Island Public Market opens.

The new courthouse and Robson Square complex are completed. The designer is Arthur Erickson.

White Rock hosts its first International Sandcastle-building Competition. Unruly behaviour by spectators closes the event in the 1980s.

W.A.C. Bennett, B.C.'s longest-serving premier, dies in his sleep at age 78.

–Hardip Johal

Dave Patterson — The Province

Colin Price —The Province

VANCOUVER, 1971 The police riot squad wades in after 2,000 young hippies gather in Maple Leaf Square for a "smoke-in" protest in favour of legalizing marijuana. They pass around a three-metre-long joint and, at about 10 p.m., the police on horseback move in with nightsticks flailing. The battle rages for three hours as the crowd responds with rocks and bottles. Eighty people are arrested in what becomes known as the Gastown Riot.

VANCOUVER, 1976 Former premier W.A.C. Bennett and his son, Premier Bill Bennett, attend the funeral of H.R. MacMillan at Christ Church Cathedral. These two men have held the reins of power in B.C. for a total of more than 30 years. A Who's Who of B.C. business and politics makes up the 400-strong congregation attending the forest magnate's funeral.

VANCOUVER, 1972 Police on motorcycles clear a path for Mayor Tom Campbell's car through demonstrators who have linked arms to protest the opening of the new Georgia Viaduct. Placard-waving members of the Committee for Transportation Alternatives respond by kicking the car and throwing things at it. "Ladies and gentlemen—and I use that phrase roughly," quips Campbell in his speech.

Ross Kenward — The Province

— The Province

Former premier Dave Barrett and his wife, Shirley Barrett, respond to cheering New Democrat supporters on June 4, 1976, after he won the Vancouver East riding in a provincial byelection.

Why doesn't Barrett end union political funds?

I read with interest Premier Barrett's comments, which were no doubt exaggerated, concerning corporate donations to the Social Credit Party. While, no doubt, there was some truth in his comments, his credibility on this subject would be greatly enhanced if he were to take some action in another area where he has some influence.

Every member of a trade union affiliated with the B.C. Federation of Labour is shaken down every month when part of his union dues is placed in the "B.C. political education fund"—a polite term for NDP slush fund! It is unlikely that more than 10 per cent of the members would voluntary donate the money—small though that amount is per month. Voting patterns indicate that probably 50 per cent of these members do not vote NDP at election time. I find it strange that unions, originally organized to rescue workers from slavery, should treat their members like indentured slaves in this particular matter.

Mr. Barrett, however, can correct this situation by prohibiting, under a special section of the proposed act on fundraising and election expenses, the diverting of union funds to a fund to be used on behalf of any political party. Then I could believe that Mr. Barrett is truly a man of principle—a true democrat, not just a New Democrat.

F.J. SULLIVAN
Campbell River, May 16, 1975

Best bet is to crack down on bad drivers

I am one of those drivers who doesn't buckle up my seat belt.

I have been driving for the past 50 years and have about two million miles behind me. I never had any points or paid traffic violation fines except parking tickets. I had brake failure three times and front and back tire blowouts at 60 and 65 miles per hour, but I always maintain full control of a vehicle I operate and thereby avoid any mishaps. Wearing a seat belt will not improve my driving, but it does restrict my freedom of movement.

The emphasis, in my opinion, should be not on mandatory use of seat belts but on responsible driving and condition of the vehicle—brakes, steering, lights, signals, tires and windshield wipers and giving right of way to all pedestrians. Proper signalling is the only way you can inform other drivers as to what you intend to do.

I suggest that if all individuals who have one or more violations were removed from the road for a period of time and were required to take driving lessons and rigid driving tests, the results could be enormous. This, too, would serve as a warning to all other drivers that if they violate traffic safety laws they would lose their driving privileges and could be required to take lessons and rigid driving tests.

Traffic laws should be amended and strengthened. Learner permits should be extended to one year. In cases of serious and criminal violations, the penalty should be commensurate with the offence—suspension of driving privileges up to life.

P. PAWLIUK
North Vancouver, April 19, 1976

Vancouver lives in glass house

Re: Eric Nicol's column of May 27 regarding the Manhattanization of Toronto. He refers to an incident where a Toronto bus driver was attacked by hoodlums, and no one went to his assistance. He suggests that at present, at least, Vancouver is free of such shocking incidents. Yet he conveniently ignores a *Province* item of May 23 with a large headline: "Woman's screams are ignored by milling crowd of shoppers." The fairly lengthy item details a sexual attack on and robbery of a woman in the Bay parkade, in downtown Vancouver on a Wednesday afternoon. Both her screams for help and attempts to attract attention by blowing her horn were ignored by passersby.

Eric Nicol displays a tendency, all too common in Vancouver, to stigmatize eastern cities, primarily Toronto. This has the regrettable effect of blinding us to our own defects.

(Mrs.) OONAGH MAGRATH
Vancouver, June 9, 1975

No herbicides!

The Port Coquitlam & District Hunting & Fishing Club strongly protests B.C. Hydro's intention to use 2-4D herbicide on their right-of-way and gas line. We ask that they refrain from using ANY type of chemical herbicide because of their known and unknown hazards to present and future generations. These chemicals have been proven to cause mutations, birth defects and cancer. No further research is needed and we cannot understand their persistent use.

BEVERLEY HOLMES
Port Coquitlam, Feb. 1, 1977

Share decision-making

If a "satellite-overview" could be taken of our collective bargaining system, it would clearly show up the anti-social aspects of the present system.

How much better it would be if a system were introduced that would remove the gap between industry and labour.

In our classless society, the existence of a gap between management and labour has become obsolete. Given the necessary qualities of leadership, an apprentice can become a captain of industry. Moreover, each citizen can become an owner of shares in almost any industry and certainly many a wage-earner takes home more in pay than what is left over for many a businessman. Rather than insisting on remaining on opposite sides (and remaining a hazard to production), the parties could sit at a round table and each company could have representatives on their board of directors. Shared decision-making has been tried and found successful in several European countries, almost entirely eliminating any desire to strike or lock out.

J.A. GROENEWEGEN
Princeton, July 24, 1975

Blame Bill

Vivienne Clarke's letter in *The Province* does her credit. Democracy is dying. For instance, we have vegetable boards, fruit, milk, egg, poultry boards, all formed to protect groups from competition and force prices up. That's not helping to solve inflation.

Our premier is to blame in allowing his ministers to ignore how things are going.

ERNEST GRANGER
Burnaby, Oct. 18, 1979

Commuter transit

I have read with interest the suggestion of "subways" or "underground railways" for the Vancouver area. I don't think much of the idea and know it would be astronomically expensive. However I have a constructive counter-suggestion. Many years ago the B.C. Electric ran an interurban tram. One route went via New Westminster as far as Chilliwack and another via Marpole and out to Steveston. It would appear that right-of-way and some trackage is still operating. I should think it would be very feasible to reinstate a "commuters' train" on this old system. Not only would it be a service to the valley, Sea Island, Lulu Island and Delta but in the summertime would be a marvelous tourist sightseeing attraction.

(Mrs.) M.S. JEWITT
West Vancouver, Aug. 8, 1974

MLA cut good example

After reading many comments on the provincial budget, I am surprised that no one has said much about the 10-per-cent cut in the salaries of cabinet ministers and MLAs.

I see this cut as a step in the right direction. More attention should be focused on it, however, to encourage further curtailments in wages and spendings.

DAN BEATON
Vancouver, April 19, 1976

Gerry Kahrmann —The Province

Vancouver, 1986

The city goes nuts for a whole summer during Expo 86. More than 22 million people visit 84 pavilions from 40 countries, nine provinces, three U.S. states and 32 corporations. Visitors sample exotic food and drink and listen to entertainment from around the globe. Expo changes the face of the city forever, leading to more relaxed liquor laws and an explosion in the demand for variety in the city's restaurants.

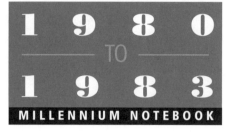

WELCOME, WORLD

BY DAMIAN INWOOD

The decade opens with a tale of two mountains.

One is Mount St. Helen's in Washington state, which scatters ash over B.C. after erupting violently on May 18, 1980, killing 58 people.

The other is Blackcomb Mountain, which opens in December in a revitalized Whistler.

That same year, the Lower Mainland is terrorized by a string of grisly child murders, leading to the arrest of Clifford Olson. Two years later, he's convicted of 11 murders and gets life in jail.

A young, one-legged cancer victim, Terry Fox, dies in 1981 at age 22 after giving up his cross-Canada Marathon of Hope fundraising run.

"Towel Power" sweeps B.C. as the Canucks go to the Stanley Cup final for the first time and then lose in four straight games to the New York Islanders.

A car-bomb explodes outside the Litton Systems plant in Toronto. A group called The Squamish Five is later jailed for the attack.

B.C. Place opens in 1983, and Premier Bill Bennett brings in his restraint package. Operation Solidarity musters 40,000 protesters at Empire Stadium.

Brian Mulroney wins the Tory leadership in 1983. He goes on to become prime minister.

Pierre Trudeau resigns as prime minister in 1984. He's replaced by John Turner.

Pope John Paul II tours Vancouver and rides in a white pickup truck around a jammed B.C. Place Stadium.

Steve Fonyo emulates Terry Fox by running across Canada to raise money for cancer research. His name is later blackened by drunk driving, fraud, assault, theft, perjury and weapons offences. He goes to jail.

Expo 86 draws 22 million people, including the Prince and Princess of Wales.

The Coquihalla Highway and SkyTrain both open and Premier Bill Bennett steps down. His successor is Bill Vander Zalm, whose pet phrase, "faaantastic," rings out across B.C.

Sprinter Ben Johnson brings pride, then shame, winning gold in the 100 metres but testing positive for steroids at the '88 Seoul Olympics.

The end of communism in Europe is heralded when the Berlin Wall falls in 1989.

The '80s end with another mountain in the news: In Montreal (Mount Royal), on Dec. 6, 1989, 14 women are killed by crazed gunman Marc Lepine at École Polytechnique.

> **Expo 86 draws 22 million people, including the Prince and Princess of Wales**

1980

Feb. 29: Jeanne Sauve is appointed first woman speaker of the House of Commons.

April 12: Port Coquitlam's Terry Fox, who lost a leg to cancer, begins his Marathon of Hope to raise money for research. He runs for 143 days, from St. John's, Nfld., to Thunder Bay, Ont., when he's forced to stop after cancer appears in his lungs. His run raises $25 million. He dies June 28, 1981, at the age of 22.

May 18: Mount St. Helens in Washington State erupts, setting off fires, mudslides and floods and killing nearly 60 people. It rattles windows in Vancouver.

May 20: Quebec votes 60 per cent against sovereignty association in a referendum.

Nov. 4: Ronald Reagan, 69, is elected U.S. president.

Dec. 8: In Manhattan, former Beatle John Lennon, 40, is fatally shot five times by crazed fan Mark David Chapman, 25.

1981

March 30: President Reagan is shot while leaving a Washington hotel. Doctors remove a bullet from his left lung. On June 21, 1982, gunman John W. Hinckley Jr. is found not guilty by reason of insanity.

April 12: The space shuttle *Columbia* takes its maiden flight.

May 13: Pope John Paul II is shot twice by escaped Turkish convict Mehmet Ali Agca, 23. The Pope survives after surgery to remove parts of his intestine.

June 21: Wayne Williams, 23, is charged with killing 28 children and young adults in Atlanta. In 1982, Williams is sentenced to two consecutive life terms.

July 29: In a fairy-tale wedding with a global audience, Charles, the 32-year-old Prince of Wales and heir to the British throne, marries Lady Diana Frances Spencer, a 19-year-old kindergarten teacher, amid pomp and pageantry in St. Paul's Cathedral in London. An estimated 750 million people around the world watch the event on television. The newlyweds ride in a gilded horse-drawn

Courtesy Apple Computer

Macintosh unveiled

In a TV ad playing off George Orwell's 1984, a group of faceless people sit in a room, listening to a Big Brother figure droning away on a large video screen. A young woman, wearing a white tank top and red running shorts, runs into the room. She flings a track-and-field hammer at the screen, shattering the Big Brother image.

With this commercial, which airs during Super Bowl XVIII, Apple introduces its new computer, the Macintosh, and throws the home-computing revolution into high gear.

One of the first 32-bit computers, the Mac gives Apple a big edge over rival IBM, until recently the home-computing champ with its line of 16-bit machines.

Spurred by the rivalry and the increasing "user-friendliness" of the machines, the home-computer industry does a booming business in 1984. The commercial—known as "1984" and directed by Blade Runner director Ridley Scott—revolutionizes advertising; it leads to the Super Bowl becoming the showcase for ad debuts.

Diana and Charles

carriage back to Buckingham Palace to begin what will become a doomed marriage.

Aug. 31: Clifford Olson is charged with nine counts of first-degree murder of children.

Oct. 6: Anwar Sadat, the Egyptian leader who made peace with Israel, is assassinated.

Nov. 14: The Canadarm, built by Spar Aerospace of Toronto, is first used in space aboard the space shuttle *Columbia*.

1982

Feb. 15: The drilling rig *Ocean Ranger* sinks off Newfoundland, taking the lives of the crew of 84.

March 26: The first test-tube twins are born to Katherine and Ian Rankin, of Oakville, Ont.

April 2: Argentine Gen. Leopoldo Galtieri

orders troops to seize the Falkland Islands. British Prime Minister Margaret Thatcher sends 100 ships to the disputed South Atlantic Falklands. Britain loses four ships. Argentina surrenders June 14 and Galtieri resigns.

April 17: Queen Elizabeth signs Canada's repatriated constitution at a ceremony on Parliament Hill.

1983

March 2: The final episode of *M*A*S*H* is watched by 125 million, the largest television audience for any non-sports program.

Sept. 1: Korean Air Lines Flight 007 is hit by two Soviet missiles, killing 269 people. The USSR says the plane is on a spy mission.

Oct. 23: The U.S. Marine HQ in Beirut is destroyed by a truck bomb. The blast kills 241 marine and navy personnel, in Lebanon as part of a peacekeeping force.

Oct. 25: President Reagan sends an invasion force to the Caribbean island of Grenada after a coup by pro-Cuban Marxists. By Nov. 2, hostilities are over.

Dec. 23: Jeanne Sauve, former speaker of the House, becomes the first woman to be appointed Governor General of Canada.

MEDICINE

A NEW PLAGUE

The AIDS epidemic officially arrives in Canada in 1983, although the first cases are later found to have occurred as early as 1980. In B.C., nearly 10,000 people have so far tested positive for HIV.

The first official AIDS announcement appears in the U.S. on June 5, 1981. The Morbidity and Mortality Weekly Report, issued by the Centre for Disease Control, reports five cases among homosexual men in Los Angeles.

A month later, 41 young men, most of them gay, have Kaposi's sarcoma and eight quickly die.

Doctors initially call it "gay-related immunodeficiency" (GRID) but the name is changed to acquired immune deficiency syndrome.

1980S TRENDS

THAT EXASPERATING CUBE

The Rubik's Cube, designed in 1974 by Hungarian architecture professor Erno Rubik, comes on the market in 1980. The multicoloured cube has six sides, each with nine squares. The aim is to make each side of the cube one colour. Mathematicians calculate this can be done 43,252,003,274 trillion ways.

NEW IN 1980
- Post-it notes, from 3M Corp.

NEW IN 1981
- MTV, the first 24-hour music channel, aimed at 12- to 34-year-olds. A Canadian version created by CITY-TV's Moses Znaimer, Much-Music, signs on in 1984.
- Pac-Man video game.
- IBM PC, personal computer.

NEW IN 1982
- *E.T.*—The Extra-Terrestrial.
- *Late Night With David Letterman,* on NBC.
- Liposuction.

NEW IN 1983
- Cabbage Patch Kids.
- Computer mouse.
- Compact disc.
- Camcorder.

NEW IN 1984
- PG-13 film ratings.
- *Miami Vice,* on NBC.
- *The Cosby Show,* on NBC.

NEW IN 1985
- Nintendo video games.

NEW IN 1988
- Prozac, from Eli Lilly.
- Rogaine, the first hair-growth drug.

NEW IN 1989
- Teenage Mutant Ninja Turtles.

WORLD EVENTS

TIANANMEN SQUARE

With brutal force, the Chinese army uses tanks to break up a Beijing pro-democracy student rally in Tiananmen Square in June 1989.

After martial law is imposed, several thousand students remain and are massacred with automatic weapons and tanks.

The death toll of up to 2,500 students brings condemnation from the West.

The next day, after the blood-stained square has been hosed down, the world's attitude towards communist China is changed forever.

The image of a lone student facing down a Chinese tank becomes a rallying cry for protests against the actions of the regime.

At the University of B.C., students build a replica of the Goddess of Democracy torn down by authorities in Tiananmen Square and still mark the event with an annual vigil to honour those killed.

SCANDAL

SAY IT AIN'T SO, BEN

Millions of Canadians sit glued to their television sets on Sept. 24, 1988, watching Canadian sprinter Ben Johnson set a world record of 9.79 seconds and win a gold medal at the Seoul Olympics. The next day joy turns to shame as news breaks that "The Fastest Man in the World" has tested positive for using a performance-enhancing anabolic steroid. He's stripped of his record and his medal.

Johnson sparks an unprecedented probe into the use of drugs in Canadian athletics. The Dubin Inquiry sits for months and Johnson admits steroid use. He later gets a lifetime ban after a second failed test and subsequently fails a third time.

Ben Johnson

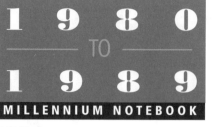

1984

Jan. 2: Oprah Winfrey makes her debut and within a month takes her Chicago talk show to the top of the local ratings. Two years later, *The Oprah Winfrey* Show is syndicated and overtakes daytime talk-show king Phil Donahue to become the highest-rated talk show in TV history.

Feb. 28: Michael Jackson wins eight Grammy Awards for his album *Thriller*, the best-selling pop album of all time.

May 8: Denis Lortie attacks people in the Quebec National Assembly with a sub-machine gun. He kills three and wounds 13 before giving himself up.

June 6: Indian troops storm the Golden Temple, held by Sikh extremists, killing about 1,000. Militants retaliate Oct. 31, when Prime Minister Indira Gandhi, 66, is assassinated. Rajiv Gandhi, her son, 48, takes her place.

July 18: James Huberty, 41, walks into a McDonald's in San Ysidro, Calif., and opens fire with three guns. A police sharpshooter kills Huberty but 20 people die.

Oct. 4: Marc Garneau, aboard the shuttle *Challenger*, is the first Canadian astronaut in space.

Oct. 12: British Prime Minister Margaret Thatcher escapes injury when an IRA bomb explodes in a Brighton, England, hotel, killing two and injuring 34.

Dec. 3: A toxic gas leak at a Union Carbide insecticide plant in India kills about 3,000 people.

Dec. 10: Anglican Bishop Desmond Tutu receives the Nobel Peace Prize for non-violent efforts to end apartheid in South Africa.

Dec. 22: Bernhard Goetz shoots and injures four black youths on a New York subway. He says they were trying to rob him. A grand jury indicts Goetz on weapons charges and he's later indicted for attempted murder. He is acquitted but loses a $43-million civil case to one victim.

1985

Feb. 20: The first cruise missile test flight takes place at the Cold Lake, Alta., base. Greenpeace protests by releasing 23 weather balloons in the missile's path.

March 11: Mikhail Gorbachev becomes Soviet Union leader. Gorbachev's reforms unleash changes that will bring down Communism.

March 21: Rick Hansen leaves Vancouver on his Man in Motion wheelchair marathon to raise money for spinal-cord research. He will travel 40,000 km through 34 countries in 26 months.

Sept. 1: The luxury liner *Titanic*, which has lain on the ocean floor for 73 years, is found in 4,000 metres of water south of Newfoundland in the North Atlantic.

Oct. 2: Rock Hudson dies at age 59. He disclosed in July that he had the AIDS virus.

An unsolved bombing

Two luggage bombs are checked in at Vancouver International Airport on June 22, 1985, by men who do not board their planes.

One bomb downs Air India Flight 182, killing all 329 aboard.

Within an hour, a second bomb explodes at Tokyo's Narita Airport, killing two baggage handlers.

Sikh extremists are blamed and a $1-million reward, the largest in Canadian history, is offered for information. It is still unclaimed.

The RCMP will spend more than $26 million investigating the bombings, which killed 280 Canadians.

— Canadian Press

Photo taken 2,000 metres down by a robot submersible shows windows in the fuselage of the downed Air India plane.

— Associated Press

Communism dealt final blow

For 28 years, it stood as the Cold War's most visible divide—a barrier of concrete and barbed wire separating the people and ideals of the East and West. So it is a stunning event when, on a chilly November day in 1989, the Berlin Wall comes tumbling down—at the hands of thousands of East and West Germans, who then clamber atop the rubble to celebrate.

Days earlier, a million East Germans gathered for the largest pro-democracy rally in the communist nation's history. On Nov. 9, officials announce that they will allow East Germans to pass through the wall to visit the West. The floodgates are open. Some use hammers to chip away at the monument to state control. The next day, all border restrictions are lifted and thousands cross back and forth.

Communism in Europe collapses quickly, one country following another. Mikhail Gorbachev had opened the gate of freedom—with such concepts as glasnost (openness), and perestroika (restructuring). In July, Gorbachev tells European leaders that the Soviets will no longer use military muscle to influence Warsaw Pact neighbours.

Less than two months later, Poland becomes the first country to transfer power to a non-communist and gains support from Moscow. By October, thousands of East Germans have fled to the West.

1986

Jan. 28: The space shuttle *Challenger* explodes 73 seconds into its flight, killing all seven crew members on board, including high-school teacher and mother of two Christa McAuliffe, the first typical citizen chosen to travel in space. A presidential commission concludes that the explosion was caused by faulty O-ring seals on the solid fuel rocket booster. Tests had shown the seals to be unreliable in cold weather, but NASA failed to heed warnings because of an "overambitious" launch schedule, the commission reports.

Feb. 27: After defeat at the polls, Ferdinand Marcos hands over the Philippines presidency to Corazon Aquino.

April 8: Movie star Clint Eastwood is mayor of Carmel, Calif.

April 28: A reactor fire at Chernobyl nuclear power station in Ukraine releases a radiation cloud 10 times more potent than the atomic bomb used on Hiroshima in 1945. After a 36-hour delay, 200,000 people are evacuated.

May 2: Expo 86 is opened by the Prince and Princess of Wales in Vancouver. Almost 21 million visit before it closes on Oct. 13

June 1: Canada's new Divorce Act comes into effect. It gives one ground for divorce—breakdown of marriage because of cruelty, adultery or a year's separation.

Nov. 13: U.S. President Ronald Reagan admits that arms were sold to Iran. On Nov. 25, the White House discloses that some profits from the arms sales were diverted to support rebel Contras in Nicaragua. Reagan says he "was not fully informed" and Marine Lt. Col. Oliver North is fired. The Iran-Contra scandal is born.

1987

March 19: Jim Bakker resigns from his TV evangelist's ministry after admitting an extramarital "sexual encounter" with a church secretary, Jessica Hahn.

May 8: Colorado Sen. Gary Hart, Democratic presidential nomination contender, drops out after it's disclosed he had an affair with model Donna Rice.

June 30: The $1 "loonie" coin goes into circulation in Canada.

Oct. 16: An 18-month-old girl tumbles into a 22-foot-deep well in her back yard in Midland, Texas. "Baby Jessica" McClure remains trapped for 58 hours.

Oct. 19: On "Black Monday," the Dow Jones industrial average drops 508 points and closes at 1738.34. The 22.6 per cent decline is the worst in U.S. history, double that of the 1929 crash.

1988

Feb. 21: After reports that he committed lewd acts with a prostitute, Rev. Jimmy Swaggart publicly confesses to "moral failure" and is directed to stop preaching for a year. On May 22, he will preach without ministerial credentials and later be defrocked.

Dec. 2: Benazir Bhutto, 35, becomes prime minister of Pakistan and the first female prime minister of a Muslim country.

Dec. 22: Pan Am Flight 103 explodes. The Boeing 747 jetliner crashes in Lockerbie, Scotland. All 259 people aboard the plane die and 11 are killed on the ground. Investigators pin the explosion on a terrorist bomb.

1989

Jan. 24: Serial killer Ted Bundy dies in the electric chair in Florida for slaying a 12-year-old girl. Investigators believe he may have killed several dozen women.

March 24: The supertanker *Exxon Valdez* runs into a reef in Alaska's Prince William Sound. Eleven million gallons of oil gush from the vessel, killing 600,000 birds and 5,500 otters and spoiling 1,600 kilometres of shoreline.

Oct. 17: An earthquake measuring 7.1 on the Richter scale rocks the San Francisco area. Almost 70 die, half of them crushed when freeways collapse.

Dec. 6: A gunman kills 14 women at the University of Montreal.

VANCOUVER, 1984
Pope John Paul II raises his hands in a salute to more than 60,000 as he travels around B.C. Place Stadium. A crowd of between 150,000 and 200,000 had greeted him at Abbotsford Airport.

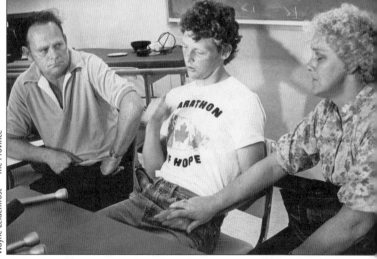

Wayne Leidenfrost — The Province

NEW WESTMINSTER, 1980 Betty Fox holds her son Terry's hand while dad Rolly looks on anxiously during a difficult hospital press conference. Holding back tears, the 22-year-old runner has just announced he is giving up his Marathon of Hope because the cancer that took his leg has moved to his lungs. Terry Fox has (pictured at left during his run) had to give up in Thunder Bay. He dies June 28, 1981, but his dream lives on. Millions of dollars are raised for cancer research as thousands across Canada run and walk every year.

— The Vatican

— Canadian Press

KELOWNA, 1987 The RCMP riot squad is called in after gangs of young people go on the rampage during the 81st Kelowna Regatta celebrations. Police use helicopters, tear gas, dogs and clubs to flush out rowdies who, for the second year running, are smashing store windows and throwing rocks and bottles. About 200 are arrested. The regatta is eventually cancelled.

1980

In April, Port Coquitlam native Terry Fox, whose right leg was amputated as a result of cancer, begins his cross-country Marathon of Hope. His efforts will raise $25 million for cancer research.

Ashes scatter over B.C. after Washington's Mount St. Helen's erupts in May.

After 32 years of construction, the nine-kilometre Stanley Park seawall is finally completed.

1981

On May 1, the diving boat *Huntress* explodes in Coal Harbour, killing two and injuring eight.

On Oct. 16, police break up a Ku Klux Klan rally celebrating Anwar Sadat's assassination.

Richmond has a record 188 rainy days in 1981.

1982

The Vancouver Canucks make it to the Stanley Cup final. They are defeated by the New York Islanders in four straight games.

Mass murderer Clifford Olson receives 11 consecutive life sentences for killing 11 Vancouver-area children. The government pays Olson $100,000 to tell police where he hid the bodies.

On Nov. 13, the dome of B.C. Place Stadium is inflated in one hour.

1983

In November, 80,000 B.C. government and education workers walk out, protesting Premier Bill Bennett's plan to curtail wages.

On Oct. 23, the Kuan Yin Temple opens in Richmond. It is North America's first authentic Buddhist temple.

1984

Vancouver's Lori Fung wins a gold in rhythmic gymnastics at the L.A. Olympics.

Mike Hamill—The Province

VANCOUVER, 1986 "See Expo and Di" reads *The Province's* front page headline as Diana pays us a visit, along with Prince Charles. Diana causes a scare when she faints during a tour of the California pavilion. "A plucky Princess Diana proved her mettle," reports *The Province*. It is later revealed that she has been suffering from an eating disorder and that her marriage is in trouble.

COQUIHALLA HIGHWAY, 1985 The rush is on to complete the new link between Vancouver and the Interior in time for Expo. Two weeks after Expo opens, a smiling Premier Bill Bennett opens the new stretch of pavement. The highway linking Hope to Peachland costs close to $1 billion—not the $375 million originally estimated. An inquiry looks into overruns amid claims of a government cover-up.

— The Province

David Clark — The Province

VANCOUVER, 1983 About 40,000 angry members of the Operation Solidarity coalition protest against Socred Premier Bill Bennett's restraint package. B.C. Federation of Labour president Art Kube calls on Bennett to restore slashed social programs. Bennett shrugs off the rally, saying it is held by NDP supporters "demonstrating against the results of the last election."

— The Province

Gerry Kahrmann — The Province

VANCOUVER, 1984 Riding the success of his chart-topping album, *Thriller*, Michael Jackson plays three concerts with his brothers at B.C. Place. More than 100,000 tickets are sold for the shows, which gross a record $5 million. "The Victory tour may be the largest road show in history, but the skinny little guy covered in sweat and glitter is the dynamo that makes it work," writes *Province* rock critic Tom Harrison.

1984 continued:

In May, a project called "Shame the Johns" is launched to move prostitutes' clients out of the West End. By July, prostitutes have moved east to Seymour Street.

A three-month bus strike hits Vancouver.

1985

In March, Williams Lake native Rick Hansen embarks in his wheelchair on an around-the-world "Man in Motion" tour. He will travel 40,000  kilometres through 34 countries and raise $14 million for spinal cord research.

A telephone answering machine with remote access is $319.95, and Ice Capades tickets at the Pacific Coliseum are $8 to $9.50.

The SkyTrain opens Dec. 11.

The B.C. Lions win their second Grey Cup.

1986

Sun Yat-Sen Gardens open in Chinatown.

1987

On Oct. 15, Queen Elizabeth II opens the Commonwealth Leaders' Conference in Vancouver.

1988

The Fraser Valley has a record June rainfall of 144 millimetres.

Forty per cent of all new B.C. homes built in 1988 are in Surrey.

1989

Science World opens May 6.

Rob Boyd achieves his third World Cup win in downhill skiing at his hometown, Whistler.

The Whalley All Stars make the Senior Little League World Series finals, but lose to the defending champs from Taiwan.

—Melissa Radler

VANCOUVER, 1981 From the air it looks like a gigantic "O" but the $126-million B.C. Place Stadium is starting to take shape. A contest to pick a name for the teflon-roofed stadium is quietly dropped, although one cab driver suggests, "the Mushroom in Bondage." Queen Elizabeth visits the stadium in March 1983 and invites the world to Expo 86. The official opening on June 19 draws only 40,000, foreshadowing a trend that will haunt the facility, which seats 60,000-plus.

BURNABY, 1988 Cars lie scattered like broken toys after the roof of a new Save-On-Foods store collapses in Burnaby on opening day. Cars on a rooftop parking lot plunge through the roof. Although 1,000 are in the store, including owner Jim Pattison, only 16 people are injured, none seriously. Full-page ads for the new $15-million megastore had boasted: "Escape the ordinary—discover the extraordinary."

Rick Loughran — The Province

— The Province

Another dark age

Gunter Light and many others may be sick of the creation-evolution controversy, but I'm astounded that people are willing to sit back and allow this regression of society. The creationists are certainly not about to drop the issue, and I don't think the rest of us should sit on the sidelines as the creationists force their way into the school system.

I agree that we are not headed for heaven, and I hope that we are not headed for another Dark Age.

LYNNE GORMICAN
Vancouver, May 19, 1981

Cart parts

Mr. Smelt suggests that customers should act as volunteer spotters and report abandoned shopping carts to the appropriate store. A good idea in theory, but has Mr. Smelt ever tried to get the phone numbers of some stores?

I recently did report to two different stores the location of abandoned carts (Woolco and Safeway). The Safeway cart remained where it was for four more days. The Woolco cart was never picked up. Its wheels were removed by persons unknown about a month after I first reported it.

Human need before human greed.

AL PHILLIPS
Kamloops, May 22, 1981

Horse sense

I am not a horse-racing fan, but it seems there's money in it—money that's needed to operate the big circular dome in the centre of the city. So, why not try horse-racing there?

R.T. BARNARD
Vancouver, April 22, 1987

— The Province

Thousands of demonstrators take part in the annual peace march through the streets of Vancouver on April 29, 1985.

Lemming march

If in some miraculous way we could discover what motivates the lemmings to join in a mass march to commit suicide, we might get some clue to the activities of the "peace" marchers. Can they really believe that if we discard all weapons and smother the Politburo with love, that they will respond in the same manner? That cold-blooded hierarchy has openly stated that its aim is to "bury" us, as they have already "buried" so many nations in Europe and Asia.

H.B. DICKENS
Ladysmith, May 1, 1985

Don't look away

I was brought up in refugee camps but never in my life have I seen anything as pathetic as the pictures of mothers in Ethiopia watching their children die of hunger before their eyes.

If today we close our eyes and ears to the plight of the Ethiopians, then tomorrow we might learn to do the same at home.

As a society we would end up paying a heavy price.

BISH BHAGWANANI
Victoria, Dec. 6, 1984

Last resort

Now that the effects of restraint are being widely felt, it is time to show compassion and introduce a government-sponsored suicide clinic—where people who feel they cannot cope any longer could at least end their lives with some dignity.

RICK BUTCHER
Burnaby, March 17, 1985

Cut from the top

After watching the *Wayne and Shuster Show* on our $700-million-a-year network, I can only shudder at the thought that this drivel may be shown beyond our borders.

No wonder Canada is perceived as a frozen wasteland.

Surely we deserve better from the CBC.

I applaud the economy cuts. I only regret that the people at the top will keep their jobs and the little guys will get laid off.

MARK BEAUCHAMP
Kelowna, April 11, 1985

Anti-porners not funny now

My husband and I once rented porn movies. I saw only the same thing again and again and again . . . sex. But all parties were willing participants. After three movies I was bored and have never watched one since. I thought that was the extent of pornography. Little did I realize there are things such as snuff movies (in which children are murdered) and films of actual rape.

I used to laugh when I saw TV shots of anti-porn demonstrators—I was uneducated in the subject. After the *Man Alive* program, I know the truth. I no longer laugh. The world and Canada must be pretty sad when this type of thing is condoned.

ROSE MARTIN,
Midway, Jan. 3, 1985

Senseless

I am sick to death of this government being made a scapegoat for every hardship and tragedy in life.

The senseless murder-suicide of the Cheng family was the result of a man's inability to cope with a job loss. No one is to blame but the man himself. We are informed that he had no debts. How many of us are that lucky?

T. YADA
North Vancouver, March 17, 1985

Sold on Albert

It looks as though it will be between the Canucks and the Maple Leafs for last place overall. Well, perhaps while the talented and hard-working teams compete for the Stanley Cup, we should challenge the Leafs for the Albert Cup—with the winner getting the first-round draft choice.

I. HANNAFORD
Burnaby, Jan. 7, 1985

(Albert was a player in a Canadian Tire commercial who prompted a rival coach to say: "I wish we had a guy like Albert."—Editor)

The real issue

I take umbrage at your editorial (Oct. 2) in which you stated that the national deficit is the most important issue in the election campaign.

The polluting and poisoning of the environment should be the most important issue. Unless drastic measures are taken to "clean up," the question of deficits won't really matter.

Environmental collapse will make it and related problems redundant.

R.H. PRINSEP
Vancouver, Oct. 6, 1988

Illusionist

Re: Comments by Charles Lynch (Jan. 24) regarding his fond memories of the pleasures of smoking, all of which he has valiantly foregone for the sake of the colour of his lungs.

I do believe that he and all those other non-smoking hopefuls jogging along with the carbon monoxide traffic are indulging a grand illusion.

MARIE RICHARDS
Vancouver, Feb. 23, 1986

— Reuters

Nagano, 1998

Ross Rebagliati wins Olympic gold in the snowboard Super G but comes close to being stripped of his medal after a trace of marijuana is found in a post-race urine test. Rebagliati, a native of Vancouver, denies he has recently used the drug. He says he must have ingested it in the form of second-hand smoke at a party with his buddies before he left for Japan. His medal reinstated, Rebagliati, 26, returns to a hero's welcome as thousands gather in the town centre of Whistler, where he lives. "Smoke a fattie for Rebagliati" read signs carried by supporters.

GOLDEN BOY

BY DAMIAN INWOOD

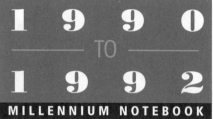

The 1990s start off being dominated by the letter 'M' with Meech Lake, the Molson Indy and the movie industry.

A country fed up with constitutional in-fighting is relieved when Brian Mulroney's Meech Lake Accord is scuttled by Manitoba and Newfoundland.

In Vancouver, the screech of rubber is legal when the first Molson Indy hits a street course around B.C. Place.

And "Hollywood North" puts B.C. third in moviemaking behind Los Angeles and New York.

After getting bogged down in a scandal over the sale of Fantasy Gardens, Premier Bill Vander Zalm steps aside in 1991. Rita Johnson is sworn in as Canada's first female premier.

Two years later, Bill Clinton and Boris Yeltsin hold a two-day summit in Vancouver, and the city's Kim Campbell becomes Canada's first female prime minister.

It's also a year when the words "Clayoquot Sound" penetrate the public consciousness. Anti-logging protests abound.

The Stanley Cup riot rocks Robson Street after the Canucks lose to the New York Rangers in the 1994 Stanley Cup final. About 70,000 descend on downtown and are dispersed by riot police firing plastic bullets.

Another black eye is the 1997 APEC conference, which draws world leaders—and crowds of demonstrators opposed to human-rights violations.

Students at UBC are manhandled and the RCMP officer who peppersprayed them is dubbed "Sgt. Pepper."

The event leads to a commission of inquiry into claims that Prime Minister Jean Chretien personally ordered the police action.

Ross Rebagliati and Gillian Guess become household names: He an 1998 Olympic snowboarder who is almost stripped of a medal after traces of marijuana are found in his blood; she a juror who has an affair with one of the accused in a murder trial.

The Quebec ice storm, the creation of Nunavut and Wayne Gretzky's retirement all make headlines.

The decade ends with boatloads of Chinese migrants appearing on B.C. shores, and the Battle in Seattle, where protesters, including some APEC veterans, rally outside World Trade Organization talks.

> About 70,000 descend on downtown and are dispersed by riot police firing plastic bullets

1990

Jan. 3: Two weeks after U.S. President George Bush sent 25,000 troops to capture Manuel Noriega, the Panamanian strongman surrenders to U.S. authorities.

Mandela

Feb. 11: Nelson Mandela, leader of the African National Congress, is released from prison in South Africa after serving 27 years on a charge of treason.

March 13: The Soviet Congress of People's Deputies repeals Article 6 of the Soviet Constitution, which gave the Communist Party a political monopoly.

June 4: Dr. Jack Kevorkian admits helping Janet Adkins, 54, of Portland, to commit suicide.

Oct. 3: Split into two countries after Nazi Germany's 1945 defeat in the Second World War, the two Germanys are formally reunified.

1991

Jan. 1: The seven-per-cent goods and services tax takes effect in Canada.

March 3: Los Angeles police officers beat black motorist Rodney King, 25. A videotape of the violence plays on CNN, showing at least a dozen officers surrounding King, landing 50 nightstick blows and breaking his skull in nine places. On May 2, 1992, violence erupts in L.A. after an all-white jury acquits four white police officers of beating King. At least 58 people are killed. In April 1993 a federal jury convicts Sgt. Stacey C. Koon and Officer Laurence M. Powell of civil rights violations in King's beating. Two other officers are acquitted.

July 24: Jeffrey Dahmer, a paroled child molester, confesses to killing 11 men and boys in Milwaukee and eating the flesh of some of them. In November 1994, Dahmer will be slain in prison.

Aug. 19: Soviet hard-liners, opposed to Mikhail Gorbachev's reforms, launch a

Turning back Saddam

For the first time since they fought in Korea, Canadians go to war in January 1991 against Iraqi dictator Saddam Hussein.

It all starts months earlier, in the early hours of Aug. 2, 1990, when Hussein invades oil-rich Kuwait.

Tensions increase Sept. 21 when Saddam, known to possess chemical and biological weapons, threatens to launch pre-emptive attacks on his Arab neighbours and Israel.

— Canadian Press

Two Canadian soldiers share water in Qatar during the Gulf War.

On Nov. 29, the UN Security Council imposes a Jan. 15 deadline for Saddam to pull out. When he doesn't, a U.S.-led coalition of 28 nations, including Canada, launches an aerial assault called Operation Desert Storm on Jan. 16.

The allies use high-tech weapons, including "smart bombs" with video cameras on their noses, to bombard Baghdad, the Iraqi capital.

Canadians watch as eerie, infra-red TV footage shows the green flashes of the nightly bombardments and as burning Kuwaiti oilfields belch black smoke.

Leading CNN's 24-hour-a-day coverage is Canadian Peter Arnett, its war correspondent. Another Canadian, Arthur Kent, becomes known as the "scud stud" for his coverage on NBC television from Saudi Arabia as missiles landed nearby.

Canadian Gen. John de Chastelain is in charge as CF-18s bomb Iraqi forces from bases in Qatar and warships are on standby in the gulf.

The war ends Feb. 28 when U.S. troops re-take Kuwait City.

About 20,000 cheering, flag-waving people welcome Canadian troops back in Toronto.

---

coup. Clambering atop a tank, Russian President Boris Yeltsin calls the takeover unconstitutional. Two days later, the coup collapses and Gorbachev returns. His power is diminished and he resigns.

Oct. 6: Anita Hill, a law professor who worked for Supreme Court nominee Clarence Thomas, tells a Senate hearing that he made lewd suggestions to her. Thomas calls the allegations "lies" and "sleaze." He is con-

Roberta Bondar

firmed by a 52-48 vote on Oct. 15.

Nov. 8: Earvin (Magic) Johnson, 32, star forward for the L.A. Lakers, announces that he is HIV-positive and that he will retire.

Jan. 22: Astronaut Dr. Roberta Bondar is Canada's first woman in space as she blasts off for a seven-day mission on board the NASA space shuttle *Discovery*.

May 9: A methane gas explosion kills 26 miners in the Westray coal mine near Plymouth, N.S.

May 22: Johnny Carson takes his final curtain call after 5,000 shows and nearly 30 years on *The Tonight Show*.

Oct. 24: The Toronto Blue Jays win the first World Series for a Canadian team.

Nov. 4: Democrat Bill Clinton becomes U.S. president with 43 per cent of the popular vote.

FILM

SPIELBERG'S SPECIAL YEAR

Director Steven Spielberg reaches new heights in Hollywood with two films as different as they could be. The first is the 1993 summer blockbuster *Jurassic Park*, based on Michael Crichton's bestselling novel about a modern-day return of dinosaurs. In December, Spielberg premieres the haunting *Schindler's List*, detailing the real-life story of Oskar Schindler, a German businessman, con man and hero who saved thousands of Jews from Second World War death camps. The movie culminates a 10-year project of the heart for Spielberg and will win Academy Awards for best picture and director in 1994.

Spielberg

SPORTS

YERRR OUTTA THERE!

Some of 1994's top sports stories remove players from competition. The National Hockey League locks out players in a dispute over rising player salaries and the lockout lasts almost half the season. Major League Baseball players walk off the field in August after team owners threaten a salary cap. For the first time since 1904, the World Series is cancelled. Just before the 1994 Winter Olympics, seedy associates of U.S. figure skater Tonya Harding try to eliminate rival Nancy Kerrigan by clubbing her on a knee. Kerrigan recovers in time and wins a silver medal at the Olympics. Harding skates miserably.

Harding

TRENDS

NEW IN 1990
- A McDonald's in Moscow
- Low-calorie fat substitute (Simplesse)
- FDA-approved contraceptive implant (Norplant)

NEW IN 1993
- Legal euthanasia, in the Netherlands
- Combat roles for women in the U.S. military

NEW IN 1994
- Conclusive evidence of the existence of black holes in space
- An all-female America's Cup sailing team
- TV series *ER* on NBC

BOMBING OF YUGOSLAVIA

After 78 days of intense and bloody NATO air strikes, the Serbs sign a pact June 8, 1999, and leave Kosovo in 11 days.

Eighteen Canadian CF-18s have taken part in the aerial bombardment of Yugoslavia. The U.S-led attacks follow reports of Serb death squads roaming villages and slaying ethnic Albanians.

U.S. President Bill Clinton calls on Balkan strongman Slobodan Milosevic to withdraw his troops. He refuses, and bombs rain on Belgrade and Pristina as 860,000 refugees flee to camps in neighbouring Macedonia and Albania.

In Vancouver, about 1,000 people rally to protest the U.S.-led bombing and to burn flags and call for an end to Canada's role.

Milosevic backs down, his country in ruins, and 800 Canadian peacekeepers go to Kosovo.

SCANDAL

'THAT WOMAN' IMPERILS CLINTON

On Jan. 21, 1998, *The Washington Post* discloses a sexual liaison has taken place between Clinton and a young White House intern named Monica Lewinsky and that Clinton has tried to cover up the affair. A stalled investigation by independent counsel Kenneth Starr is alive again.

Clinton issues an angry denial. "I did not have sexual relations with that woman," he says, in a TV clip that will haunt him. But rumours of oral sex and a blue dress that is stained with the president's DNA persist.

On Aug. 6, Lewinsky testifies before a grand jury and on Aug. 17, Clinton testifies on a closed-circuit video link between the White House and the grand jury.

He admits later on TV: "I did have a relationship with Lewinsky that was not appropriate ... I misled people, including even my wife. I deeply regret that."

Starr's report is made public. On Oct. 8, the House approves impeachment but the Senate acquits Clinton on Feb. 12, 1999.

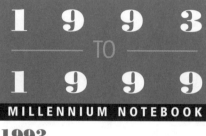

1993

Feb. 26: A bomb in an underground parking lot in New York's 110-storey World Trade Centre kills five people and hundreds suffer from smoke inhalation.

March 29: Catherine Callbeck is the first Canadian woman to be elected premier, in Prince Edward Island.

April 19: An armoured vehicle smashes through a front wall of the Branch Davidian compound of cult leader David Koresh and his 95 followers in Waco, Tex.

At 12:15 p.m., flames and smoke pour from the compound. Only nine cult members survive the inferno. At least 17 children are killed.

April 30: Tennis champion Monica Seles is stabbed by a fan in Hamburg, Germany.

June 25: Brian Mulroney turns over the office of prime minister to Kim Campbell, Canada's first female prime minister.

Sept. 13: Palestine Liberation Organization chairman Yasser Arafat shakes hands with Israeli Prime Minister Yitzhak Rabin after the two sign a peace accord on the White House lawn.

1994

Jan. 17: An earthquake measuring 6.6 on the Richter scale kills 57 people and causes $15 billion US in damage in California.

Jan. 21: Lorena Bobbitt, who cut off part of her husband's penis, is found not guilty of malicious wounding, by reason of insanity.

March 4: Canadian actor John Candy dies in Mexico.

March 26: Pop icon Michael Jackson marries Elvis Presley's daughter, Lisa Marie Presley. They will file for divorce less than two years later.

April 26-29: South African blacks, voting in national elections for the first time, sweep African National Congress leader Nelson Mandela to the presidency.

May 6: England's Queen Elizabeth II and French President Francois Mitterrand open the $15 billion Channel Tunnel, which connects England to Europe.

May 10: Serial killer John Wayne Gacy, 52, is executed by lethal injection in Joliet, Ill., for the sex slayings of 33 young men and boys in Chicago in the 1970s.

Sept. 12: Legislation comes into effect making health warnings on cigarette packages sold in Canada larger and more visible.

1995

March 20: A nerve-gas attack during rush hour in a Tokyo subway kills 12 and injures 5,000.

April 13: CBC announces it is dropping *Front Page Challenge*, on TV since 1957.

May 18: The trial of Paul Bernardo and his wife Karla Homolka, accused of the murder and torture of Kristen French, 15, and Leslie Mahaffy, 14, begins.

July 17: Christine Silverberg is the first woman police chief of a major Canadian city, Calgary.

Nov. 4: Israeli Prime Minister Yitzhak Rabin, 73, is gunned down at a peace rally. 1996

1996

Feb. 19: The $2 "toonie" coin goes into circulation.

March 20: Brothers Lyle and Erik Menendez are convicted of the 1989 killings of their wealthy parents in California and sentenced to life in prison.

April 3: U.S. agents arrest the "Unabomber," Theodore Kaczynski. Since 1978, he has killed three and injured 23 with letter bombs. In 1998, he pleads guilty in exchange for a life sentence.

July 19: Flooding caused by torrential rains kills 10 people and leaves 2,000 homeless in the Saguenay region of Quebec.

Nov. 5: President Clinton is re-elected, defeating Bob Dole.

Dec. 26: JonBenet Ramsey, a six-year-old girl who has been in beauty pageants, is found strangled in her home in Boulder, Colo. Suspicion falls on the parents.

1997

Jan. 16: Ennis W. Cosby, only son of comedian Bill Cosby, is fatally shot on a freeway ramp in Los Angeles.

Feb. 4: O.J. Simpson is found liable in civil court in the slayings of his ex-wife, Nicole Brown Simpson, and her friend Ronald Goldman. A jury awards $33.5 million US in damages.

March 26: With comet Hale-Bopp at its closest to Earth, 39 members of Heaven's Gate religious cult commit suicide in Ran-

Like a candle in the wind

Canadian television viewers are jolted when a report interrupts programming on the night of Aug. 30, 1997. Sombre news anchors confirm that Diana, Princess of Wales, 36, has been in an automobile accident in Paris.

Within hours, officials at a Paris hospital confirm that the estranged wife of Prince Charles is dead.

A chauffeur-driven Mercedes-Benz carrying Diana and companion Dodi Fayed is followed into a tunnel by news photographers on motorcycles.

Travelling at more than 95 km/h, the car goes out of control and hits a wall. Killed with Diana are Fayed and chauffeur Henri Paul. Bodyguard Trevor Rees-Jones is critically injured but survives.

Images of the tunnel and the Mercedes, its front end demolished, will remain seared in the public consciousness for days.

A week later, millions of Canadians get up before dawn to watch Diana's state funeral on TV.

They watch as Diana's sons, Prince William and Prince Harry, walk with their father behind the horse-drawn funeral carriage.

In a moving service, British Prime Minister Tony Blair reads from the Bible, Elton

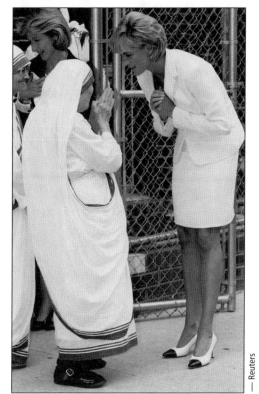

Diana, Princess of Wales, bows to Mother Teresa at a charity function in the Bronx, New York, on June 18, 1997. Both died later that year.

— Reuters

John sings a new rendition of Candle in the Wind, and Diana's brother, the Earl of Spencer, delivers a passionate, sometimes scathing eulogy.

At British consulates across Canada, memorials to Diana spring up as part of the worldwide grieving for the dead princess.

Anger centres on the papparazzi who have hounded Diana from the first days after her 1981 engagement to Prince Charles was announced.

Diana's death brings to an end a chapter of sniping within the royal family. Her brother opens a memorial at the family home in Althorp and thousands visit it.

---

cho Santa Fe, Calif. They believe that the comet is trailed by an alien spaceship that will take them to a higher plane of existence.

May 31: Confederation Bridge opens to traffic between Prince Edward Island and the mainland.

July 1: After 156 years of colonial rule, Hong Kong is returned to China by Britain.

July 9: Danielle House gives up her Miss Canada International title after pleading guilty to assaulting her boyfriend's ex-girlfriend.

July 23: One of the most intense manhunts in U.S. history ends when 27-year-old Andrew Cunanan commits suicide in

Miami Beach, Fla. The gay gigolo is sought in the July 15 killing of fashion designer Gianni Versace and for slaying four other men.

Sept. 5: Mother Teresa, the nun who dedicated her life to helping the sick and destitute of India, dies of a heart attack at age 87. Born in Macedonia, she founded the Order of Missionaries of Charity in 1948. The order would open 600 ministries in 100 countries. Mother Teresa's work earned her the Nobel Peace Prize in 1979.

Oct. 13: When the brakes fail on a seniors' sightseeing bus, 44 die when it crashes into a ravine at Les Eboulements, Que.

1998

Jan. 6: A crippling icestorm leaves over one million people without power for 10 days in Quebec and eastern Ontario.

March 6: The Ontario government announces that three surviving Dionne quints, Annette, Cecile and Yvonne, are accepting $4 million in compensation for the nine years that they spent on display at a tourist theme park .

March 24: At the Academy Awards, Canadian director James Cameron's *Titanic* wins 11 Oscars, including that for best picture.

Aug. 7: Bombs explode at U.S. embassies in Nairobi, Kenya, and Dar es Salaam, Tanzania, killing at least 257 people and injuring thousands. On Aug. 20, the U.S. launches retaliatory missile strikes against a chemical plant in Sudan and terrorist camps in Afghanistan.

Sept. 2: Swissair Flight 111 crashes into the ocean off Peggy's Cove, N.S., killing all 229 on board.

Dec. 16: U.S. President Clinton orders four days of air strikes against Iraq after Saddam Hussein fails to co-operate on UN weapons inspections.

1999

April 1: The Territory of Nunavut is created, with Inuit leader Paul Okalik as first premier.

April 18: Wayne Gretzky, No. 99, retires after 20 years in pro hockey. He's set records in every scoring category.

July 16: At dusk, John F. Kennedy Jr. is piloting a small plane from New Jersey headed for Martha's Vineyard, Mass. With him are his wife, Carolyn Bessette, and her sister, Lauren. The plane never arrives. The search lasts five days. On Sept. 21, the three bodies are found on the ocean floor inside the single-engine plane.

Aug. 17: One of the century's largest quakes strikes Turkey. More than 17,000 people die.

Oct. 20: Retail chain Eaton's closes its doors after declaring bankruptcy.

VANCOUVER, 1994 Lui Passaglia is lifted by delighted teammates after he kicked the last-gasp winning field goal that gave the B.C. Lions the Grey Cup. Passaglia kicked the 38-yard game-winner with no time left on the clock to give the Lions a 26-23 win over the Baltimore CFLers at B.C. Place Stadium.

VANCOUVER, 1990 Faye Leung poses in one of her trademark hats. Leung is the realtor at the centre of the sale of Fantasy Garden World, which leads to the resignation of Premier Bill Vander Zalm Apr. 2, 1991. Vander Zalm resigns after conflict-of-interest commissioner Ted Hughes found he was in breach of his own rules in the sale of his theme park to Taiwan billionaire Tan Yu. Leung later weeps as she is sentenced to 15 months imprisonment for stealing $45,000 and taking $115,000 in secret commissions from investors in connection with a failed condominium development in Surrey. Vander Zalm later becomes leader of the B.C. Reform Party and loses a Delta by-election.

Gerry Kahrmann — The Province

— Canadian Press / CBC News

VANCOUVER, 1997 This image, taken from CBC-TV is forever linked with the APEC protests at UBC, when police pepper-sprayed students in November 1994. The students had set up along a route taken by APEC leaders to protest human-rights violations in several countries. RCMP Staff Sgt. Hugh Stewart wins the media title "Sgt. Pepper" after spraying students and TV cameras. The police action later results in a lengthy inquiry, after protesters claim the police were personally directed by Prime Minister Jean Chretien.

— Victoria Times Colonist

VICTORIA, 1997 Makund Pallan comforts his daughter Suman Virk, mother of murdered teenager, Reena Virk, at a memorial service. In an incident of youth violence that shocked the country, 14-year-old Virk was beaten and drowned under the Craigflower Bridge. Eight teens were charged. Of those, six teenage girls were sentenced for assault causing bodily harm and the remaining two, Warren Glowatski and Kelly Ellard, who were 16 and 15 respectively at the time, received life sentences for second-degree murder. Glowatski has no chance of parole for seven years and Ellard for five—the minimum.

1990

Vancouver's first Molson Indy is held on a track at B.C. Place. A track worker is killed when he attempts to push-start a car.

The Order of British Columbia goes to rock star Bryan Adams.

Vancouver is named the third largest film-production centre in North America after Los Angeles and New York.

1991

Rita Johnson becomes B.C.'s first female premier after Bill Vander Zalm resigns in disgrace.

1992

Rossland skier Kerrin Lee-Gartner wins the gold at the Albertville Winter Olympics.

1993

In early April, U.S. President Bill Clinton and Russian leader Boris Yeltsin hold a two-day summit in Vancouver.

Environmentalists hold an anti-logging rally at Clayoquot Sound.

In June, Vancouver's Kim Campbell becomes Canada's first female Prime Minister.

The Supreme Court votes 5-4 to deny Victoria's Sue Rodriguez, who suffers from Lou Gehrig's disease, the right to an assisted suicide.

U.B.C. Professor Michael Smith wins the Nobel Prize in chemistry.

A dismal record is set this year when 357 people in B.C. die of drug overdoses.

1994

On June 29, Premier Mike Harcourt announces plans for an overhaul of B.C.'s ferry system, including the construction of three high-speed ferries.

Victoria hosts the Commonwealth Games from Aug. 18 to 28. Guests include Queen Elizabeth II and Barbara Streisand.

On Sept. 17, GM Place opens in Vancouver. The Vancouver Grizzlies play their first game at the new stadium in October.

In November, the B.C. Lions win their third Grey Cup in 30 years.

NEW AIYANSH, 1998 Nisga'a elders arrive at the Gitlakdamix recreation facility in New Aiyansh for the historic signing of the Nisga'a treaty. The treaty was preceded by more than 100 years of negotiations. Its signing in July 1998 was followed by criticism from the provincial Liberals, who called it "unconstitutional."

VANCOUVER,1993 On election night, Oct. 25, ousted Prime Minister Kim Campbell keeps up a brave front for her disappointed supporters as the news of Jean Chretien's Liberal landslide flows in. Campbell became the first prime minister since McKenzie King in 1945 to lose a home riding and her Tories were reduced from a majority government to two seats in parliament. "Gee, I'm glad I didn't sell my car," she quipped.

MONTREAL, 1998 A family grieves. Former Prime Minister Pierre Trudeau, his son Sacha, ex-wife Margaret Kemper and son Justin weep as they leave a Montreal memorial service for Michel Trudeau. Michel, 23, died in an avalanche that swept him into B.C.'s Kokanee Lake during a back-country ski trek with friends. His body was never found. Kemper later announced she was separating from her second husband of 15 years, Ottawa real-estate agent Fried Kemper, partly because her grief at the death of her son led to the breakup of the marriage.

— Canadian Press

Below: **VERNON, 1996** This Okanagan town is stunned as it buries a family slain by an estranged husband. After a 15-month separation, and with his wife Rajwar Gakhal pursuing divorce, accountant Mark Vijay Chahal kills his estranged wife, her parents, four sisters, brother and brother-in-law. Two others at the home are shot but recover in hospital. The massacre occurs on Good Friday at the Gakhal home as the family prepares for the wedding of Rajwar's younger sister the next day. Chahal then shoots himself. Afterwards it is learned there has been a history of abuse before the murders. Rajwar told Vernon RCMP that Chahal beat her but that she wanted to report it for information only. She had also been getting nuisance calls from Chahal, who denied making them. In total, she had complained four times to Vernon police.

— Canadian Press

Jon Murray — The Province

1995

Armed Natives occupy a private ranch in Gustafsen Lake. A standoff with the RCMP lasts more than a month.

During a Vancouver speech, Cuban dictator Fidel Castro calls Americans "scorpions, vipers and snakes."

Premier Mike Harcourt, taking the fall for the so-called "bingogate" scandal, resigns.

1996

A new $260-million international terminal at Vancouver International Airport opens May 1.

On June 19, B.C.'s first astronaut, Robert Thirsk, flies into space aboard the space shuttle *Columbia.*

Roman Catholic Bishop Hubert Patrick O'Connor becomes the highest ranking Catholic in the world to be convicted of rape when he is found guilty in the assault of a native girl in Williams Lake.

1998

Avalanches across B.C. kill nine people in a 24-hour period on January 2.

Former B.C. juror Gillian Guess is sentenced to 18 months in prison for obstruction of justice.

On July 15, B.C. signs a treaty with the Nisga'a.

1999

Since July, 599 men, women and children have arrived in B.C. illegally from China aboard four separate vessels.

On Aug. 21, Premier Glen Clark resigns amid accusations of misconduct. In a scandal dubbed "casinogate," Clark is accused of attempting to help a neighbour and contractor get a casino licence in exchange for work on his house.

–Melissa Radler

VANCOUVER, 1994 About 70,000 unhappy fans gather around the intersection of Robson and Thurlow after the Vancouver Canucks' loss in Game 7 of the Stanley Cup final. When a man tries to walk on trolley wires and falls into the seething mass, he triggers a chain of events that unleashes a full-blown riot. An ambulance dispatched to pick up the fallen daredevil is surrounded and rocked by the crowd. Riot police wade in to clear the intersection. They fire teargas, violence breaks out and the situation rapidly gets out of hand. Rioters smash 2,000 windows and cause about $250,000 in damage. Police arrest 50 and about 175 revellers and eight police are injured. Charges are laid and claims of excessive use of force made against the police.

Ric Ernst — The Province

Ric Ernst — The Province

Ric Ernst — The Province

'Social misfits' to blame for riot

Like others, I watched the newscasts of the disgusting, brainless scum who trashed downtown Vancouver Tuesday night.

I had walked down Robson Street at mid-afternoon and felt the anticipation of the game. There were many spontaneous displays of support for the team. Noisy but peaceful. But there was also a strange undercurrent of something ominous. That evening, the slime crawled out from under the rocks and saddened a city's soul.

Blame a generation raised on violent movies and TV? Blame their parents for sparing the rod? In the end, the only ones to blame were the social misfits themselves.

As someone said on a radio broadcast before the game: "Nobody asks where you're from or cares what religion or colour you are. We are all Canucks fans today."

The human garbage tried to ruin that feeling. Never again! The small, spontaneous gangs trying to provoke violence in the future will be met by a new, much larger gang … The Majority. Join up.

Bob Benger
Richmond, June 16, 1994

— The Province

Rioters attack vehicles and businesses after the Canucks lost the 1994 Stanley Cup.

Tobin all wet

Fisheries Minister Brian Tobin recently stated that three million missing salmon is no "disaster."

Perhaps it would be equally no "disaster" if Mr. Tobin sought an alternative occupation.

Paul Davey
Vancouver, Oct. 11, 1994

Seeing is learning

Steveston Senior Secondary School is said to be the most overcrowded school in Richmond. We have to walk to portables, we have text books dated 1982, it takes us 10 minutes to get to classes and we have to line up to use washrooms. As a student at Steveston, this is what I hear every day and it has got me thinking.

Since I was eight, I've done a great deal of travelling. I've been to seven different Third World countries. I can remember walking through the streets of Penang, in Malaysia, and seeing children younger than me selling pop in old tin shacks. I remember driving through the streets on the Indonesian island of Bali, and seeing children walking home from a half-burned old barn that served as a school.

I remember asking a kid in Bangkok, Thailand, what grade he was in. He told me he'd never been to school.

Recently, a group of students from our school travelled to Guatemala to reunite Guillermo Perez with his family. (He was an exchange student at our school for a year).

This group of students had the nerve to complain about our school when they returned.

I'm content with textbooks that have a few scratches on them, with having 10 minutes between classes, with our brand-new comfortable portables.

Besides, the most important thing I've ever learned certainly isn't taught at Steveston.

Courtenay Heard, Grade 12,
June 21, 1995

Spice Girls spread happiness

Too bad *The Province* reviewer didn't enjoy the Spice Girls' show ("The Spice Girls just want to have funds").

My daughters Jacqueline, age 11, and Julia, age five, and their 11-year-old friend Kayla and I most certainly did.

From where I was sitting in the ninth row on the right in section 105, the show was fantastic.

I don't think I have ever seen my girls so happy, not to mention the other happy little faces I saw around me.

May I suggest that the next time your reviewer goes to a concert that isn't their cup of tea, get up out of your seat, go outside and give your ticket to a fan and make her or his day.

The Spice Girls' message is positive and fun. We need more of that in this world.

Lisa Champion
Port Moody, Aug. 16, 1998

Phooey to feng shui

I see that Richmond city council has hired a feng-shui expert to assist it in its new city hall design. This comes at the same time they are cutting $1.5 million from other areas of the budget. My kids will lose recreation programs at the local community centre and arts and historical opportunities at our cultural centre, my roads will be in poorer repair and there will be fewer police and firefighters in case of an emergency. But if I go to the new city hall all will be in balance, according to an ancient Chinese superstition.

I hope the mayor consulted with his astrologer to make sure all these things were announced on the most auspicious days.

Patricia Wong
Richmond, Nov. 16, 1997

Inconceivable

Stop the insanity already! I can't think of anything more irresponsible, selfish and immature!

How could anyone create a human being for a lark? That's what's happening around the world in preparation for the Year 2000 ("Couples did everything conceivable," The Province, April 11, 1999).

People should put more consideration into having a child than they do into the purchase of a pair of shoes. But it seems that many folks are ready to jump into bed nine months before January 1, 2000, without any forethought.

They may not be ready to be parents. They may not be able to afford a child. They might not even like kids. But they're all ready to try to have the first baby of the Year 2000. If this is a popular trend, we're going to end up with a baby boom that produces a very large number of unplanned, unwanted, unloved babies.

Children are too precious to be created on a whim. This baby boom is going to cause overcrowding of hospital maternity wards, overcrowding of elementary schools five years later, overcrowding of high schools 13 years later, etc.

If you want to do something frivolous for New Year's, buy a pair of shoes without even trying them on!

Jerry Steinberg
Vancouver, April 14, 1999

Bill's boots

Why are the media searching so relentlessly for reasons why Premier Bill Vander Zalm should resign as leader? Why don't they also ask caucus members who have brought disgrace to their party if they plan to do the honourable thing and depart?

Sure, Vander Zalm has great difficulty defining conflict of interest. But let's not forget that not too long before Bill got mixed up with those unsavoury Socreds, he was an innocent, ruddy-cheeked young fellow who sold flowers and went around with a girl who wore a band around her head. After all, the manure on Vander Zalm's boots didn't all come from the Fantasy Gardens stable. A lot came from tramping around the Socred zoo.

Tom A. Graham
Vancouver, Dec. 30, 1990

Let them eat smoke

I am a smoker who is finding it more and more difficult to find a place to light up—McDonald's being the latest. I was heartened to learn that meat-eaters are 40 per cent more likely to develop cancer than vegetarians. As I have been told countless times that it is my fault for rising medical costs because of my smoking, it would be only fair to start screaming at all meat-eaters for raising our medical costs. I can hear the cries of indignation about personal freedoms and government intervention—from the same people who have been treading all over my rights. Don't get me wrong—I love meat—but I've had so much abuse about my smoking that I'll be more than happy to see those holier-than-thou non-smoking meat-eaters take some heat.

M.A. France
Qualicum Beach, July 4, 1994